A Grown-Up Lent

When Giving Up Chocolate Isn't Enough

Joanna Leiserson

A Grown-Up Lent

When Giving Up Chocolate Isn't Enough

Joanna Leiserson

Forward Movement
Cincinnati, Ohio

Morehouse Publishing
New York • Harrisburg • Denver

Forward Movement
www.forwardmovement.org

Morehouse Publishing
NEW YORK • HARRISBURG • DENVER

A Grown-Up Lent

When Giving Up Chocolate Isn't Enough

Introduction

I love Lent! It begins on Ash Wednesday when the world seems to change. Even the air around us seems muted, for just this day, as if the planet itself were listening. I love being reminded that the whole universe, including the human "We Are Invincible" species is dust, and to dust it shall return. And most of all, I love the fact that the retail world has not yet figured out how to market this day. I have not seen even one **Ash Wednesday Mattress Sale** or one **Ash Wednesday Super Special On Knee Pads** (75 percent less cushioning for the truly penitent!).

When I was young, my friends gave up sweets, chocolate, and soda for Lent. One creative boy gave up swearing. Then, every year, the Lenten season ended with a veritable feast of sweets, chocolate, soda, and colorful language. It was as if the act of fasting and self-denial merited them a reward from God of the very thing they had given up.

Not growing up in a church-going household, I was always baffled when friends would ask, "What are you giving up for Lent?" My question was much simpler: "What is Lent?"

When I was in grade school, my friends gave me their very best grade-school theology. The ashes and Lent and the giving-up of things are what you do to be sorry for your sins between

Ash Wednesday and Easter. Later I learned the ancient traditions and customs of Ash Wednesday and Lent. But, as with many traditions, we sometimes keep the customs but forget the reasons. I wonder whether that is true today as we continue to ask that old grade-school question: What are you giving up for Lent?

Maybe what we really need to give up for Lent this year is our grade-school theology. Maybe it is time for Lent to grow up.

We can begin by asking the right question.

The questions for the season of a grown-up Lent, are not "What will you give up for Lent?" or even "What will you do for Lent?" but rather "Who will you be in Lent?" and even "Whose will you be in Lent?"

The easy answer is that we are created to be people of God, and we are created to be God's. But what does it mean to be people of God in today's world? Perhaps this year is a time to explore how to be a child of God, but a grown-up child of God, giving up a superficial approach to Lent and exploring in deep and meaningful ways what it means to connect with God in a secular, post-modern culture.

In the next several weeks, we will ponder how spiritual practices such as fasting, self-examination, prayer, and meditation on scripture might be surprisingly provocative, challenging, counter-cultural, and even subversive—just as Jesus was. Some of the meditations suggest additional reading of a parable or other words of Jesus; the scripture citations are offered.

May you have a joyful, holy, grown-up Ash Wednesday and a joyful, holy, grown-up Lent.

Ash Wednesday

Stardust

One day, a girl came to church, acc[ompanied by her] parents. It was Ash Wednesday. Wh[en it was her turn] to have the ashes imposed on her forehead in the sign of the cross, the priest said to her, "Remember that you are dust, and to dust you shall return."

She went back to her seat, crying. Later, her foster mother, who loved her very much, asked her why she was crying. She answered, "All my life, people have told me that I am dirt. I never expected the church to tell me that too!"

During the Ash Wednesday service, we lament our sins and acknowledge our wretchedness before God. We kneel before God as sinners, unable to commend the life of prayer, peace, and love that God calls us to live. And we are reminded by the ashes where we come from. But is it dirt? Are we dirt?

It is tempting to soften or even ignore the more difficult parts of Ash Wednesday in order to make our Lenten journey more palatable to us. After all, we are more accustomed to words of comfort and reassurance in church. But when we do this—when we close our ears to the harshness of the language, deny that it applies to us, inwardly tone down the message that calls for us to lament our sins and acknowledge our wretchedness—we lose the heart of Ash Wednesday and so move into Lent with a watered-down map of our journey with Christ.

The heart of this holy day is not how loudly we lament our sins and acknowledge our wretchedness, as important as that

3

for our own truth-facing. The heart is not even the [...] on our foreheads or the dust from which we came and to [whi]ch we shall return. The heart of Ash Wednesday is not Ash Wednesday. This day is not the end but the beginning.

The heart of Ash Wednesday is an invitation to go deeper into the heart of God. The whole point is not that we are dust but that we are precious, beloved children of God. The whole point is that we are precious enough to God that God would send God's only Son to redeem us and to reconcile us to God. The point is not that God wants us to be buried in ashes but that God wants us to be buried with Christ—and then risen with him. God desires not separation but relationship with us, not the death of sinners but life for us sinners.

It may help to know where the dust comes from, whereof we come and to which we shall return. Here's where:

In the far reaches of the universe a very long time ago, an old star dies, in an explosion that sends its atoms across millions or even billions of light years. Eventually the dust created by this exploded star ends up in our little corner of the universe. That dust becomes the building blocks for this world, our fragile earth, and for life, including us.

That we are made up of the remnants of dying stars should bring us to our knees in gratitude for the miracle of our creation by our Maker, who is so infinitely creative to have us born out of mighty stars. That we are then loved so much that God gave his only Son to walk with us on this earth and give himself for us is a gift beyond compare. "Remember that you are dust, and to dust you shall return." We are made from dust. But we are not dirt. We are dust, and not just any dust. We are stardust.

Thursday after Ash Wednesday

Deeper than Dust

One summer, as the result of a wrong turn on the way from San Francisco to New York, we found ourselves crossing through the southern Nevada and Utah desert rather than tooling along on the comfortable highway that everybody else takes to cross this part of the country.

After we filled up on gas at the edge of the desert, there was a bumpy two-lane highway. The first sign we saw said, "**Next Gas Station In 103 Miles.**" It was two hours before we passed a car going the other way.

When evening came, we stopped somewhere and camped for the night. The Nevada desert is much like how I would envision the wilderness where Jesus went after he was baptized, led by the Spirit. Perhaps it is also like the wilderness the Israelites wandered through between the Red Sea and the Promised Land. The Nevada desert was not sandy but rocky. There were no trees, only a bunch of shrubby little bushes dotting what in a better mood one might call "the landscape." Here and there, I came upon some bones of a large animal that either died of thirst or was killed by an even larger animal. It didn't take long in this kind of place to start thinking about what you need to survive—and what you don't need. This is not a place for spending four days, let alone forty days or forty years. When you are in the wilderness, stripped of the usual physical, emotional, social, and cultural comforts, and when you are vulnerable and exposed, what is left of you?

How would you answer the questions: Who am I? What makes me live?

When the Israelites emerge from the wilderness after forty years, they finally know who they are, where they have come from, how they got there, and who brought them there. They know that they are God's beloved people, and that it is by God's grace that they have arrived. When Jesus emerges from the wilderness after forty days, he too comes out knowing who he is, where he comes from, and what he has been sent to do.

Sometimes life gives us wildernesses like this—places in our lives where we doubt ourselves, face an uncertain future, test ourselves, and then find out who we are. But the church also gives us a kind of institutional wilderness, which we call "Lent." On Ash Wednesday, we are encouraged to remember that we are dust, and to dust we shall return. In the following weeks, we are invited to go deeper—deeper than dust—to the One who made us from dust. For forty days, we can wipe away the excesses of our daily life and find out what's left of us: who we are, where we come from, and who brings us here.

Are we wandering nomads—or the Bride of Christ? Are we orphans and slaves in Egypt—or sons and daughters of God? In the wilderness, we will find out. As we seek our answers, may we always remember that we are dust, and to dust we shall return. We are also God's beloved ones, and to God we shall return.

Friday after Ash Wednesday

Things that Pass Away and Things that Endure

Grant us, Lord, not to be anxious about earthly things, but to love things heavenly; and even now, while we are placed among things that are passing away, to hold fast to those that shall endure...
Collect for Sunday closest to September 21,
The Book of Common Prayer, p. 234

I want to introduce you to Mrs. Winchester, who made a tangible monument to the idea of life as a dead end. Sarah Winchester was the widow of the Winchester Rifle owner, living around the turn of the twentieth century. After her husband died, a medium told her to build a home for herself and for the spirits that were killed by Winchester guns and were seeking revenge on her family. The catch was that she could never stop building. Only continuous construction on the house would appease the spirits. As long as she was building, she would live. As soon as construction stopped, she would die.

Mrs. Winchester moved to San Jose, California, and for twenty-four hours a day, every day for thirty-eight years until her death, carpenters hammered away. In the end, they built a home of 160 rooms. There are staircases that lead to ceilings or to nowhere. Doors open into brick walls or empty space. A window is built into the floor.

This house, now known as the Winchester Mystery House, is an architect's nightmare, but the house was designed not so much to live in but rather to put off dying in. It stands today as a reminder of somebody who got the earthly and the heavenly turned around. Because she lost sight of what "eternal life" and "living forever" mean, she squandered the last four decades of her life trying to avoid dying. It's a house full of dead ends—for someone who saw life as a dead end.

We can laugh at Mrs. Winchester's misjudgment, partly because her delusion was so enormous and partly because the house itself stands as a visible illustration of her misspent life. But we should not be too quick to judge. It's not always so clear cut, knowing what is passing away and what will endure. We don't usually mistake a house for eternal life, but we often mistake the good life, the materially comfortable life, for the life of salvation. And we often mistake earthly life for the only life there is, even though it will pass away.

We are indeed placed among things that are passing away. We live in a box called "Earth," and it is labelled "PERISHABLE." But we are called to live for heavenly things, for peace, mercy, compassion, reconciliation, and justice. We are called to follow Jesus, whose self-giving love is the "heavenly thing" that will always endure, and the example to which we are to hold fast. When we do so, we will not feel compelled to build a Mystery House, for our faithful life will be home to the greatest Mystery of all eternity.

Don't TXT and Plow

Jesus said, "No one who puts his hand to the plow
and looks back is fit for the kingdom of God."
LUKE 9:62

An important part of a Lenten discipline has to do with focus. It's important to keep an eye on what you're really about. When Jesus begins his final journey toward Jerusalem, he meets some would-be followers on his way. But they don't want a full-time commitment. They have other things to do as well. "Let me take a little time off first, before I start working for you." "Let me work part-time. I can't make a full-time commitment."

And Jesus answers, "Don't text and plow at the same time! You'll never get there that way!"

It's important for us to keep our eye on what we are really about. Remember the bumper sticker, "Honk if you love Jesus." The next one was closer to the real point: "If you love Jesus, work for justice." But now I see "If you love Jesus, honk. If you want to meet him right away, text while driving." How will you be able to do God's work if you're always distracted?

When I moved from Washington state to Ohio, the drive took me through Montana, Wyoming, South Dakota, Iowa, and Illinois. America is vast and interesting, and all the states want you to stop and stay for a while, because maybe you'll like it so much, you'll end up living there. There are the natural wonders

9

Glacier and Yellowstone National Parks, Devil's Tower, the Mississippi River. But I have to credit South Dakota for trying the hardest to attract—or distract—the traveler. Every mile, it seems, has a marker or billboard. Come to Mount Rushmore! Visit Wall Drug, the biggest drug store in the world and home of the jackalope! Visit the Corn Palace, made entirely of corn! The home of Laura Ingalls Wilder, the birthplace of Hubert Humphrey! Deadwood, hometown of Calamity Jane and Wyatt Earp! Where was I going anyway?

Our world is full of billboards that distract us from God's kingdom. We live in a multi-tasking society that tugs at our time and tries to squeeze more of our attention each day.

C.S. Lewis once likened our earthly life to a rest stop, a road attraction on the way to the kingdom. On this stop, you get lots of chances for a preview of the final destination, and it's tempting to take a detour. And even the church is just a halfway house to the kingdom—a place to prepare for life with God, to care for the broken and lead people to fulfillment of God's kingdom. But watch out for spiritual billboards—our goal is not the Corn Palace but God's kingdom. They're very different places and not to be confused.

First Week in Lent

Fasting, Self-Denial, and
Better Things to Give Up than Chocolate

1 Lent: Sunday

A Grown-up Lent:
Nothing to Be Morose About

I have heard a lot of Lenten promises, and many get broken, not just in practice but in spirit. This is especially common when we don't know why we are making these promises. I promise to give up smoking, or eating chocolate, or my daily vanilla latte. I promise to give up laziness and to work out more. Why? Without a spiritual foundation, without a deep-in-your-bones faith, these promises start looking like New Year's resolutions, only better because they last just forty days.

But we take our season of Lent from the story of Jesus and his forty days in the wilderness. What happens to him? He goes to the wilderness to fast, and while weak, hungry, and lonely, he is tempted. He draws upon scripture and what it teaches him about God to resist those temptations. And then he comes out of that wilderness physically weak but spiritually stronger. He is now confident in his identity, his place in the world, and his mission, because he has the knowledge of God's loving, abiding presence deep within him. Jesus now has the deep-in-your-bones faith that

on away, drives the devil away, because the devil
at bedrock faith in God. And I believe that Jesus'
he tempter helped to strengthen his faith.

talk about devils much anymore. But we still
struggle with our faith. And the Church invites us to struggle.
That is the invitation of the Church during Lent. As we seek to
restore and renew our relationship with God, we are encouraged
to use our struggles with temptation in order to build up our
faith. When we come out at the end of our time in the wilderness,
we emerge with the knowledge of God's loving, abiding presence
deep within us.

Some people think we should be morose and miserable during
Lent because it's a time of penitence, being aware of and sorry for
our sins. But Jesus tells us that when we fast, when we practice
self-denial, we should put on a smile. And here's why I think he
tells us that: so often we fail to resist temptation, we keep trying
and failing, we keep falling down. And every time we fall down,
we are pulled back up again by God's love, mercy, and forgiveness.
That's nothing to be miserable about. It's the Good News—the
Gospel. In our struggles with temptations, in our weaknesses, I
see signs not so much of our failure as imperfect human beings.
I see signs of God's hope in us as redeemable, redeemed children
of the kingdom.

Let us be delighted to draw closer to God who blesses us with
every good thing that we need. We have just begun a wonderful
season of connecting to our Maker and our Redeemer. God asks
us to give up our self-indulgent appetites and ways, our blindness
and indifference to human need, and our tendency to forget about
God's love and mercy. May we enjoy every minute of this season.

1 Lent: Monday

Oblivious Eating

How shall we fast? Why fast? Just because Jesus did? Just because people fasted in the olden days? Because it's the tradition and the church tells us to fast? Perhaps when a Lenten fast has come down to merely giving up our favorite foods, it would be natural to doubt that it has any meaning.

But fasting is meant to be part of a spiritual practice that puts us into right relationship with God. When practiced intentionally to foster both self-awareness and self-forgetfulness, fasting takes away our unhealthy relationship with ourselves and our own unfaithful habits. As we are surrounded by culinary abundance, how can we fast well, justly, and meaningfully, in a world where so many people struggle even to eat?

Perhaps we might think about fasting as a way of connecting ourselves not only to God but also to the world around us. God did not create us to eat, drink, and live alone. A right relationship with God is also connected with a right relationship with our fellow creatures on this planet. Even if you were the only human left on this earth, you would still be part of a web of relationship with the flora and fauna of the earth on which life depends. Every time we put food on the table, we become part of that line of connection to others—good or bad, just or unjust, ethical or unethical.

As Lent becomes a time for restoring right relationship with God and with those around us, a Lenten fast can make us aware of, and pay attention to, those relationships that connect us—from the riches of the earth to the food on our table—and to those on whom we depend to feed us.

Think of each meal, each Lenten fast, as a meal in which we get in touch with our shared humanity. Even if we eat alone, we eat in communion with others who eat. And when we are aware of our connection, then we dine together, even in spirit, and we share a common bond. We not only share our food and drink, we also bring our stories, raise a toast to our dreams, thank God for our blessings, welcome new family members, and remember old friends. When we dine together, we make sure that everyone has enough food and no one hoards all the good stuff. It is a tough thing to enjoy a meal next to someone who is hungry.

The table of shared food is also a place for reconciliation, for forgiving and making peace, because it is much too hard to sit around a table and eat with enemies. And it is a place to bring new acquaintances and fashion them into family or friends, because dining is not something we can do well with strangers.

As we eat each meal, let us give up eating unawares, so that we might enrich connections—to God and to one another as fellow companions on this journey toward God's great and beloved community.

1 Lent: Tuesday

Indifferent Eating

We have gotten used to eating rather than dining. This is, after all, a society of "lean cuisine," fast food from drive-through diners, frozen TV dinners, and Atkins diets, after all. It's also a society sometimes too busy to dine. We eat while working. We carry our coffee cups around with us instead of sitting and enjoying a warm beverage.

But more than that, we have grown unfamiliar with the very foods we eat. I was an adult before I knew what a Brussels sprout plant looked like. I had never seen a farm. When my daughter, as a young adult, first set eyes on a cattle farm, her description made me think of the farm as a kind of "Matrix for cows," remembering the film about the pods where the humans were harvested by the millions, not able to live individual lives.

For some of us growing up in urban or suburban environments, we do not know where our food comes from, and who the people are who work to bring us our food. Even as adults, we are not aware of how our meat and vegetables are grown or harvested. So, in a way, we still have a grade-school understanding of how we fit in the food production chain. We see the meat in the store and buy it, without asking how it came to us.

Perhaps it is time to begin connecting to the world again, starting with the most basic thing—the foods we eat. This time of Lent may be an opportunity to give up indifferent eating, and thus indifferent living.

A Lenten fast that goes deeper than giving up coffee may lead you to ask: Is the coffee in your morning cup grown by workers who can go home and feed their families with what they earn? A Lenten fast that goes deeper than missing an evening meal might lead you to ask: Are the eggs you eat for breakfast laid by hens that can walk on grass and eat what they were created naturally to eat? Is the meat you have for dinner part of an animal that was allowed to feel the sun on its back, stretch its legs, and walk in a field? Is the barbequed pulled pork in your favorite restaurant processed by a company that treats the live animals mercifully and its workers compassionately?

A grown-up Lenten fast that truly restores us to God and to one another has less to do with giving up something and more to do with giving pause. A grown-up Lent takes that pause and puts it into action, giving up foods or practices or habits that are contrary to a beloved community of God.

We are intimately connected through the Internet—at least technologically if not spiritually. Perhaps we can use our invincible human technological connections to learn more about our connections to the foods that we eat. Find out how the animals raised for our use are treated, whether humanely or cruelly. Find out whether the methods used to keep fruits and vegetables healthy will keep the earth healthy as well. Find out whether the living conditions and wages of workers at farms and processing factories are just or unjust. And then eat what is just and merciful, fast from what is unjust and cruel. This ethical approach to eating and fasting puts us in touch with our fellow humans and with the rest of God's world and leads us to become wiser stewards of God's creation.

1 Lent: Wednesday

Cooties

When I was in fourth grade, we had a case of cooties in our class. Not the whole class, but one day someone pointed to a new boy and said he had cooties, and that was it. Whenever he came near us, we ran away from him. The next year, it was someone else who had cooties. Cooties weren't exactly contagious, but we acted as if they were, and we isolated anyone who was said to have cooties by not playing with him—in other words, by isolating him from the community. Rich kids, popular kids, and athletes seem to have been immune to cooties. Sometimes a brave boy or girl would make friends with the cootie carrier, and then he or she didn't have cooties anymore. It was as if the very thing that was denied to the cootie carriers was what cured them—companionship. It's as if cooties were stopped by the very acts kids avoided—contact and community and friendship.

It isn't until we get older that we know cooties are not an embarrassing disease but rather a social construct. We made it up. It was a very childish thing to do. But I suspect cooties continue in our adult lives, even though we think we have outgrown that demeaning game. We just have different words and categories for cootie-fying people.

We still have social constructs that divide and subvert the community of God. They're just different constructs. The trouble is that when we cootie-fy people for whatever reason or by whatever means—whether it's leprosy in the old days, or segregated schools, or rednecks, or Muslims, or ghettoes—we subvert and undermine the sacramental world that God made. We try to keep our less-fortunate residents out of our nice neighborhoods. We keep the poor squeezed into two or three rundown areas that we can bypass without being touched by their despair. By cootie-fying them, we can keep them out of sight, out of mind.

But Jesus had them in mind. Jesus came to heal the broken-hearted, and to heal a broken world. He came to bring the sacrament of life back to a world that had forgotten how to see God in all things and to love their neighbors as themselves. He came to heal all cootie carriers. But he came also to heal all those who would put away the lepers and the cootie carriers, those who would turn their backs on the poor and the vulnerable, those who reject the community that God first created out of love.

Once that boy with cooties had a single friend, he didn't have cooties anymore. The game was over, and the kids grew up. For the sake of God and for our community, maybe it's time for us to grow up too.

The Bejeweled Cros

You know that among the Gentiles those wh
as their rulers lord it over them, and their great ones
are tyrants over them. But it is not so among you; but whoever
wishes to become great among you must be your servant, and
whoever wishes to be first among you must be slave of all.
MARK 10:42-44

When I went to the circus-like promenade of Venice Beach in southern California with my teenage daughter, she noticed my pewter cross necklace. "You need to hide that cross," she said. The Christian symbol, she hinted, was not welcome here.

In our culture where Christianity is both dominant and sometimes domineering, the cross too often becomes a symbol of arrogance and superiority. When Christianity becomes not a light for the world but an icon of hatred and condescension, it's time to hide that cross.

But the cross that held Jesus was not that cross. I am sure Jesus never envisioned a cross made of diamonds, worn as a piece of jewelry. I am sure Jesus never envisioned that his message of humility, compassion, mercy, forgiveness, and servanthood might sometimes be forgotten and give way to acts of oppression, harm, and damnation to those of other faith traditions. So it is time to hide that cross, when it is a symbol not of service and servanthood, but of pride and superiority.

hen Jesus told us that to become his followers, we need deny ourselves and take up our cross and follow him (Mark 8:34), I don't think he was predicting his own death. There were plenty of crosses standing around in the outskirts of Jerusalem to make the point. Lugging your own cross to your own brutal execution is a pretty powerful metaphor for self-denial. Carrying your own death tool has to require a complete denial of yourself and your natural will to live. To do it willingly means to agree to live not for ourselves and our own preservation, but for God, to be a servant for God rather than a lord over others.

That is a hard lesson. In some ways, our culture has become a culture of lords, and Christianity has become the dominant culture. We have been guilty of "lording it" over others, and of being tyrants over the "unworthy," and those of other faiths. But maybe it is time for our culture to grow up, to learn how to be servants again, and to hide the symbol—and practice—of superiority that our faith and our own Lord warned against.

And then we can take out the real cross, made not of pretty stones but of our own arms spread out to welcome and to embrace. Now that's a cross.

1 Lent: Friday

My Own Personal Jesus

When I was a child, I was taught to give my heart to Jesus, committing to Jesus as my personal savior.

Centuries have passed since God sent Jesus into the world to proclaim the kingdom, since Jesus healed and preached the Good News of the kingdom, since Jesus was crucified and raised from the dead. As we move from Jesus of history to Christ of faith, and then from Christ of faith to Christ the exalted Son of God, we often lose track of the kingdom of God as our goal on this earth. In our quest to hold Jesus in our hearts, we sometimes forget to pursue the kingdom and its values—justice, liberation from oppression, compassion, welcome, forgiveness, and reconciliation. And when we forget these values, we distance ourselves from those to whom the kingdom was proclaimed: the poor and the oppressed, the sick and the suffering, and those unjustly treated. We still believe in these values—after all, Jesus told us to. We believe in Jesus. We love Jesus. But this is not enough.

To commit myself to Jesus as my personal savior is not entirely false, but the commitment, when taken alone, may be misleading. When we see faith and change of heart as a purely inward process, what good does it do? If I just believe in loving others, even if I do nothing to express this belief in action, am I still faithful to Christ?

Christian love, mercy, and compassion are not "feelings." Christianity is not a romantic notion. Love is an action. I don't need to be in love with that neo-Nazi who cursed me and spit in my face. But when a few minutes later, I see him skidding and then crashing his motorcycle on the street, I do need to love him by helping him. Perhaps the feeling will come. But the act of mercy is needed.

Compassion as a purely inward process is nice but weak. It may even be harmful to our faith. Compassion as an inward faith deceives us into thinking it alone constitutes a saved life, while in our outward life, we uphold values of success, competitive struggle, productivity, and achievement.

The theologian Johann Metz talks about how we might live out an "empathetic mysticism of open eyes." In other words, our faith is most true when we open our eyes to the world and see the needs and sufferings of the poor, when we reach out to the poor and the suffering. Our faith is most true when we reach out to them with the hope of the reign of God and the mystic love of Christ, who was crucified for us and stands with all crucified people of the world.

Now that's a grown-up faith.

1 Lent: Saturday

The Evenly Divided Cake

Laborers in the vineyard
MATTHEW 20:1-16

Fairness is a concept that is familiar to anyone who has ever raised children—or to anyone who has ever been a child, for that matter. The cake that needs to be cut into identical pieces, right down to the number of chocolate chips on top, seems to be a tradition passed down in every family from generation to generation. On the other hand, I never hear the complaint "It's not fair!" from anyone who has won first prize.

When we talk about fairness, we assume that resources or money or attention are limited, and a generous portion to one will result in a meager portion to another—a zero-sum equation. Think about that chocolate cake again. It would not be necessary to take a measuring tape to each piece if there was an infinite supply of chocolate cake. We could just take what we wanted. But if we see life as some kind of contest for power, wealth, and fame, we will always be looking for things that are not fair—that is, situations in which we feel we are not given our just desserts. We want to get the best grades, the best job, make the most money, and own the nicest home. We strive to get ahead, we "look out for number one," we complain when favors go to someone we think less deserving than ourselves.

Jesus challenges our concept of fairness in this world and makes it irrelevant in the kingdom of God. In the parable about the employer and the day laborers, the kingdom rejects normal transactional business and pays everybody equally, no matter how much they worked. I suspect some of the people in the audience walked away from Jesus that day, shaking their heads in confusion or disgust. The parable offends our sense of fairness; many people would have a hard time justifying such bizarre labor practices.

But God does not play by our laws of economics. In fact, God makes a lousy bookkeeper—spreading wealth indiscriminately, giving Larry Latecomer the same paycheck as Esther Earlybird. Life lived under the reign of God is ruled by a God who is generous to a fault, a God whose generosity offends us and baffles us. God's mercy and generosity are simply beyond our calculations of what justice is, and beyond our wildest imaginings.

As long as we project onto God our earthly standards, we will continue to be confused, or even resentful, of God's heavenly standards. No, God is not fair. God is generous. God is lavish. God is a God of abundance. The only thing this has to do with economics is the realization of how costly this love has been for God. God's sacrificial love, in Christ's death and resurrection, turns our economics upside down and makes our cries for fairness cheap indeed.

We should be grateful that God does not transact heavenly business by our standards. If we were rewarded according to our deserving, if we were partners in a transaction with God to negotiate our entrance fee into heaven, all of us would be Larry Latecomer. It's more about God's forgiveness and generosity than about our deserving.

What if the kingdom is a place where we don't get what we deserve (thank God!), but rather what our loving God wants so much to give us? What if God's infinite love and grace and mercy, all of it, is poured out on each of us, and no matter how much you get, all of it is still available to me? What if everybody gets the best seat in God's kingdom because we all get the place prepared especially for us? God's desire for goodness and mercy extends to us, even when we are confused, skeptical, half hearted, or even wicked. What if we were able to extend that same goodness and mercy to others? The good news is that God's grace is so great and so surprising that it is there for us no matter how late it is in the day—whether we are on the deathbed, in the jail cell, or after repeated failures. We do not need to earn it. We just need to hold out our hand and receive it in order for it to do its life-sustaining work. Even as the sun sets on this life, it is never too late to accept God's grace.

Second Week in Lent

Self-Reflection in an Unreflective World

2 Lent: Sunday

Growing Up in the Hall of Mirrors

The Hall of Mirrors looked like a fun excursion. My sister and I gave our tickets to the ticket man and went inside.

The Hall of Mirrors is a maze of passageways that takes you from the entrance to the exit, with walls made up of nothing but mirror and glass. To "take you from the entrance to the exit" started out as the obvious goal and soon turned into a desperate hope. For half an hour, we wound our way through that maze. We had to touch the walls to make sure we were going through doorways rather than hitting glass. We got turned around by the multiple mirrors all around us. Finally we saw the light to the outside, and after a long, desperate time going in and out and around openings to get to that light, we finally reached it. In triumph and relief, we stepped out through the doorway and were met by—the ticket man.

After almost an hour in that room, we had ended where we had begun—at the entrance to the Hall of Mirrors.

John the Baptist came to "make straight a highway for our Lord." Jesus came to lead us down that highway toward God's kingdom. But sometimes our lives feel more like a Hall of Mirrors than a highway to heaven. We know where we want to go, we even see the end ahead of us, but we keep hitting obstacles, bumping into our own image, and getting in our own way until finally, we end up just where we started!

Before we leave home, we sometimes check ourselves out in the mirror. Is my coat full of lint? Have I forgotten to comb my hair? Do I have a milk mustache? Maybe it makes sense periodically to examine our spiritual selves also. Do I see myself in the image of God? Is my life becoming a reflection only of myself and my way, rather than God's way? Am I walking God's path or wandering in my own personal Hall of Mirrors?

We are often urged to find our own way in the world. But God calls us to God's way. Sometimes we know where God wants us to go, but we just don't know how to get there. Sometimes we don't even know what God wants us to do. Often we get stuck by our own mirrors that say, "This is you." And often, the mirrors are the culture around us, a culture that says, "Life is about me." Maybe we can use the Hall of Mirrors to look at ourselves and the direction that we are going, to make sure that we do not end up where we began but rather find that highway where we will be met by the Light of the World.

2 Lent: Monday

Spiritual Fibrillation and Course Corrections: How Not to Land on the Wrong Planet

When the first spaceships shot out of earth's gravity and were sent to the outer reaches of the solar system, they received periodic course corrections. Without regular course corrections, the spaceship could have crashed into Mars, or missed a turn, or even ended up on the wrong planet.

In The Episcopal Church, the invitation to a "holy Lent" calls us to a period of "self-examination and repentance." Some of us prefer fasting and self-denial. The idea of fasting and self-denial is easier to grasp. What is self-examination? And when coupled with repentance, is self-examination just another way of burdening ourself with guilt, or making ourselves feel bad?

In a culture that is relatively analytical—we analyze everything—we tend to shy away from looking at our spiritual selves. Perhaps it's because we are afraid that we will come up short and find ourselves lacking in spirituality. Then we might need to make difficult changes in our lifestyle.

In other parts of our life, we engage in self-examination all the time. When I am driving, I make corrections in my steering so I don't hit guardrails or endanger the cars driving near me. When I go fishing, I constantly throw the fishing line into different parts of the water, or change the bait, making little corrections in my fishing, in order to find the best place to catch fish.

On a larger scale, we question our life goals—whether our job fulfills us, whether we have enough saved for college or retirement or a new car. In life situations both small and large, we ask: What am I doing right? What can I do better? Have I been true to my goals? Have I strayed from what I want to do or be?

On a more personal scale, our own body engages in self-examination all the time. Our body regulates our breathing based on our activity. The body makes sure that the heart beats regularly, its various muscles in sync to create a strong, regular heartbeat that keeps us alive. One of the ways in which the heart fails happens when the muscles become unsynchronized and uncoordinated, and the person suffers from cardiac fibrillation.

Self-examination in Lent is a spiritual course correction. The Church gives us this chance, I think, just in case we can't do it regularly without being prodded. A spiritual life without regular course correction is in danger of suffering from spiritual fibrillation—our spiritual heart beating uselessly, weakly, unreflectively, and unintentionally.

To examine our spiritual life is not so much to be shocked by our sins—it's part of the human condition not to be perfect, after all. On the other hand, the practice of self-examination gives us the opportunity to look honestly at ourselves, knowing that God also looks honestly at us but loves and forgives us, even when we start heading toward spiritual guardrails and fishing in all the wrong places.

2 Lent: Tuesday

Normal Life in the Tombs

Jesus heals the Gerasene Demoniac
LUKE 8:26-39

Jesus meets a man filled with demons. The man falls down before Jesus, and Jesus drives out the demons, sends them into a herd of pigs, and restores the man to himself.

The people of the city—what do they do? Instead of being happy that one of their people—someone's son, brother, or neighbor—is normal again, they get scared and run Jesus out of town. Now that's the scary part. Jesus heals a man, sends his demons away, and the people are afraid—of what? The man's life is changed forever, totally different. The demons are gone. Only the good guys are left.

But the good guys ask Jesus to go away. The good guys are filled with fear of the one whom the decrepit demon-filled man called "Son of the Most High God." What makes them so afraid? Is it because they saw that Jesus expelled someone's demons and they want to keep their demons? Are they afraid their lives would be changed too and are not sure they want change? Are they afraid that Jesus will see their imperfections? Maybe they don't want to admit that they have demons too.

When I meet Jesus, will I be afraid he will see how unspiritual I am? Do I really want to be transformed from my "normal" life?

It reminds me of the time I was asked to give a short talk once to a group of psychiatrists. I was really nervous because I was afraid that when they met me, they would see how neurotic I was!

Transformation is a hard thing. Once we answer God's call "Here I am!" with our own "Here I am!" we can't just go on with our old normal anymore. God asks for more, and that can be scary and feel threatening to what we are used to being. Normal is familiar. So we convince ourselves that we need our demons—the powers that keep us from God, that hold Jesus at arm's length. Think of the demons as the keepers of our safe life, the protectors of our status quo. They protect us from God—God's power and God's holiness, which are more than we can bear.

Our demons are those parts of us that so helpfully disguise our rebellious, unfaithful tendencies. They are those parts of us that help us live with the way things are—including whole systems of injustice and oppression.

What if God came and offered to take away all my past resentments and grudges against various jerks in my life? What if God came and offered to take away all the pride that keeps me from feeling foolish, or humiliated, or embarrassed when I do something stupid? What if God offered to take away all my excuses about why I got mad and kicked the dog, or why I don't want to forgive that egghead who blasted me in public last week? What if God took away my sense of respectability so I could volunteer at the shelter instead of going to the gym? Would I welcome that new life, or am I afraid of giving up my normal life?

It may be that, contrary to what we would think, "normal" is not what God wants of us. "Normal" is keeping God at a distance.

"Normal" is the city folk who ask Jesus to leave them. "Normal" is a spiritual tomb that shelters a contentment with an everyday, untransformed, inert existence.

Maybe God wants us to be less "normal" and more like the man in the tomb—someone who, despite being dirty and homeless and possessed of demons, has the courage to fall on his knees before Jesus and be transformed. Like so many of the gospel stories, maybe the good guy is not who we think it is. Maybe the good guy is the one who starts out looking bad to us, but who has the humility, the nerve, and the openness to reach out to God as God reaches out to him. Think of that! Our role model is a man with demons, who lets Jesus liberate him from the tombs that had been his normal and give him a new normal, transformed by God.

May we also be willing to give up our demons, our status quo life, our normal, and let Jesus liberate us.

2 Lent: Wednesday

All My Barns

The rich fool
LUKE 12:13-21

"What shall I do with my money? I'll just build bigger hiding places! Then I will have enough saved up for many years to come!"

Now, what's wrong with saving for retirement? Financial experts tell us that we need to save our money so that we'll have enough to live on when we are older. Security for the future is better than the prospect of living under a bridge when I retire, or living off my children's earnings. Perhaps I am being defensive. Later on, Jesus says, "For where your treasure is, there your heart will be also" (Luke 12:34). Is my heart with my retirement savings? Is my passion squirreled away in my portfolio?

Jesus tells a story about a rich man who hoards his belongings. With no immediate need for them, and no place to put them, he tears down his warehouses and builds bigger ones. Maybe we are not like this man. Maybe we don't accumulate enough stuff to necessitate building new houses or sheds to warehouse them. What's the use of buying so much that we need to store it out of sight? And with the ready availability of food, we don't need to hoard food, either.

But I still accumulate and love my things. It's hard not to want to have nice possessions, especially when I see them on billboards, commercials, and the Internet. I have given in to buying more clocks, more scarves, more drinking glasses than I can use.

Jesus does not condemn possessions. However, he warns us against our passion for stuff overshadowing our passion for God, confusing material contentment with spiritual gladness, mistaking what fuels our greed for what feeds our soul. When does my desire for the good life sabotage my faith?

The line is crossed when my faith becomes a virtual faith, a purely inward feeling—believed but not lived, felt but not acted on, like watching a reality show about myself. The line is crossed when my contentment and comfort lead me to distance myself from the struggles of others, when I find myself sliding toward indifference or forgetfulness about those outside my comfortable home. And most of all, the line is crossed when I start to think about my material comfort more than I think about God. Am I as passionate about God as I am about my home? Can I love my things and love my God at the same time?

The rich man in Jesus' story tells himself, "Soul, you have enough to last you!" He believes his material riches will sustain his soul. Not so. The true riches that will sustain his soul are God's gifts of love, compassion, and mercy. Those are the riches that need no big barns or warehouses, for they are worthless when hoarded, yet priceless when shared. May we always know the difference.

2 Lent: Thursday

Our Memories, Holy Memories

During World War II, my father was a young, love-struck army soldier. His equally love-struck fiancée, my mother, followed him and his troop as they transferred from one place to another. One day he called and told her he'd heard a rumor about an upcoming secret troop movement. "It's only a rumor, and it's top secret. But if you don't hear from me in two weeks, go to Sioux City and wait for me there." So two weeks later, my mother traveled to Sioux City by herself, checked into a hotel, and waited. A few days later, she got a call from my father. His troop had indeed been moved there, and when he arrived and finally got a weekend pass, he went to a phone booth and looked up the hotels. Starting with the letter A, he called every hotel in Sioux City until he got to the Lincoln Hotel, where my mother was staying, faithfully waiting for his call.

This story of young love was told to us over and over again. It, and other memories, were not just part of family history; they were part of our identity.

As we turn more and more to electronic, passive entertainment, I hope that we do not lose the stories and the memories that form us. As God's people, we are formed by the stories of God's people as told in the Bible—that great love story between God and us. Those stories too were told over and over again, and then finally put into writing to be preserved and told for generations to come. The writers probably never envisioned their stories would still be heard two and three thousand years after they themselves had long been dead.

An important part of telling stories is their role in building, healing, and preserving relationships lost through death or distance. When we have lost a loved one, we preserve their spirit and their presence among us by remembering stories about him or her. During a time of loss, these stories have the power to heal our grief.

Stories—happy and sad, funny and embarrassing, proud and even humbling—offer ways for me to acknowledge who I am and what brought me to where I am now. When we remember and tell our stories as a part of self-examination on our journey to God, they become holy memories and holy stories. They become part of the story of God's people, the biblical stories expanded to encompass generations and generations of people living in the larger love story between God and us. As we surround ourselves with TV stories, may we never forget our own.

2 Lent: Friday

Squandering Right

The Parable of the Dishonest Manager
LUKE 16:1-9

We enter the manager's life as he is caught squandering his employer's property. He's not necessarily a bad guy or an embezzler. At work, he spends more than he should on office supplies, buys too many computers, fun software, and the latest audio equipment. He squanders his time texting his friends or sitting at the desk reading the *Wall Street Journal* all morning long. He may squander his own property as well. Maybe he can't go to the mall without coming out with a bag full of tools and accessories for his gas grill. Or maybe he buys extravagant gifts for his family. Or he might squander his free time, spending hours staring at the TV or smart phone. When we don't know what's important, it's easy to fritter our life away. It doesn't take an act of deliberate will—just a slow, easy slide.

But getting fired wakes him up. The man thinks, "I'm dead unless I do something about this situation." Getting fired wakes him up to what's important to him—his standing in the community, his reputation, and his livelihood. He keeps these things in sight as he sets about arranging his future. And so he is saved from disaster. Maybe he even stops being a big spender.

But being a big spender is not the sin here. Jesus was also a big spender. Like God, Jesus squandered love, forgiveness, and healing. There was nothing economical about Jesus' life, or even his death, for that matter. Some thought that he used it all up, so there was nothing left for himself at the end—especially when he ended up on the cross, crying out, "My God, my God, why have you abandoned me?" But with God, there is no fear of running out of God's love. There is nothing frugal about God's love. It so overflows that it raised Jesus from the dead and raises us up from death also.

If you know what you're living for, and if you are living for God, then you can afford to be extravagant. You can spend as much as you want, fritter away as much as you want—on love and forgiveness. And if God catches you squandering love and forgiveness or being a big spender of mercy and kindness, I am sure that God will not fire you!

2 Lent: Saturday

Running Out of Fish

When I was five years old, my parents took me to the annual fishing derby at the local lake. I caught seven smelt in three hours. When I was eight, I caught 132 smelt and won the contest on the girls' side, being crowned Fishing Derby Queen. The Fishing Derby King caught 238 fish.

Hundreds of children entered the fishing derby every year, until one year, the lake ran out of fish. We had thought there was an endless supply of fish to be caught, but we were wrong. So the fishing derby was cancelled, and the lake was left to try to replenish itself.

When we participated in the contest, we would catch the fish, toss it in a bucket, put more bait on the hook, and then throw the fishing line back in. At the end of the derby, we brought our buckets to the judges, who counted the fish and then threw them away. Thousands of smelt met their end in this shameful, meaningless way.

"For our waste and pollution of your creation, and for our lack of concern for those who come after us, accept our repentance, Lord," we pray in our Litany of Penitence (*The Book of Common Prayer*, p. 268).

We didn't know then what harm we were doing to the lake, let alone to the little fish that are just as much a part of God's creation as we are. We are just beginning to see ourselves as partners rather than as consumers of the planet and its other creatures.

We have a long way to go. I still find myself buying products without knowing if they come from sustainable resources. I look at pictures of hills from which every single tree has been cut down, of mountains made up entirely of unrecyclable trash, and of smoke billowing from factories. I know that somewhere in those pictures, I am there. My life depends on the wood that comes from those trees. My lifestyle is reflected in the plastic products that I use and throw away. My living room is decorated with products from the same factories that emit toxic smoke and chemicals. My Lenten self-examination must include my part in the waste and pollution of God's creation. Just as my body is made up of water, protein, and other chemicals, so my lifestyle is made up of this good earth's precious resources.

Eventually the lake opened back up for limited fishing. The little smelts are back, and we promise to take better care of them this time.

Third Week in Lent

Prayer and Keeping Sabbath

3 Lent: Sunday

A Grown-Up Sabbath

And God rested on the seventh day
from all the work that he had done.
GENESIS 2:2

God commanded us to honor the sabbath. This is one of only ten commandments, which highlights the importance of a day of rest. Sabbath was so important that even manna didn't fall on that day.

Hundreds of rules about sabbath in the Hebrew scripture, and the conflicts between Jesus and the Pharisees about working on the sabbath, reveal how difficult it has been to live out the true meaning of a sabbath rest ever since its beginning.

We have not improved from those early struggles. As Christians, the only thing we generally agree on is that the sabbath day has moved to Sunday, honoring the first day of the Lord's Resurrection. But how are we at keeping it holy?

We have smart phones and the Internet that keep us in touch with the office 24/7. We don't want to get behind. We don't want to miss out on the latest news. An uncertain economic environment makes us insecure about our jobs, so we respond by working longer and harder. Employers cut back on workers while expecting those remaining to take up the slack, thus creating pressure for us to keep up or be fired ourselves. How can we rest when we are expected to work harder than ever to earn a living?

We want Sunday rest to be the opposite of work, so we schedule our play on Sundays. We go to the movies, play baseball, or take a drive. But are play and recreation the purpose of sabbath? Do we find the meaning of sabbath in picnics and paintball?

The Pharisees had rules for keeping sabbath to help us understand work and play. The trouble is that observing these rules sometimes became more burdensome than the work itself. America's Blue Laws, which banned shopping, the purchase of alcohol, and other "non-religious" activities, often ended up being more oppressive than liberating. And in today's secular and pluralistic society, we can no longer in good conscience impose our Christian standards on a multicultural population. Like the biblical rules, such laws sabotage the spirit of sabbath, basing it on rules rather than on God. So what is the sabbath spirit?

Many of us grew up learning the rule, "Don't work on Sundays." But the simple rules about playing and not working no longer apply in this complex society in which play and work are so intertwined, and even religious observance is complicated.

A grown-up sabbath takes the world around us into account, being mindful of our needs and expectations, and then teaches us how to navigate the spiritual journey within that culture. A grown-up Sabbath is about mindfulness—a spiritual wifi that, at least for one day, can tune in to God and put work on hold. And then, we may learn how to keep God tuned in even when we are working, thus outwitting the wifi ethos.

3 Lent: Monday

Virtual Prayer

Prayer can be an easy thing to do. That's both good and bad.

I might pray with the best intentions: "Lord, help drug addicts recover." Or I might pray: "Lord, we pray for the victims of the flood last week." "Lord, we pray for the hungry and the destitute." "Lord, give food to the poor and healing to the suffering." To pray for others is to foster awareness of sin and suffering in the world.

Sometimes, we stop there. And when we stop, we allow ourselves to avoid responsibility for the ills of the world by shifting the responsibility for action onto God. Just how is this food to be delivered to the poor countries? Do I just think it, pray for it, and it will appear—just like that? That's grade-school theology. Corporate prayers—the prayers of the gathered church community—are not meant to replace our call to serve and act for the kingdom. But if these prayers replace action we can take to alleviate these ills, they are useless and possibly harmful because they prevent us from doing something about the problems we are praying about. They become "virtual prayers," disassociated from the reality of our life and our world.

Our intercessory prayers are meant to be spoken commitments, not merely inspired language. Sometimes we catch ourselves feeling the prayer itself is enough. "We pray for all who govern and hold authority in the nations of the world, that there may be justice and peace on the earth" (*The Book of*

Common Prayer, p. 387). But when we are sent forth at the end of worship, do we go out and work for justice and peace on the earth? Or do we go out and do nothing—tolerating the way things are, maintaining the status quo, unconsciously holding up a system that reinforces poverty, injustice, and oppression?

Prayer can be an easy thing, but acting on our prayers challenges how we act in the world. May our prayers foster in us not only awareness but also responsibility, so that our prayers are meaningful, our actions reflect our prayers, and our daily lives reflect the reign of God. When we shift from virtual prayer to transforming prayer, we will have a grown-up prayer life indeed.

3 Lent: Tuesday

My Worship is Better than Your Worship

I used to look down on contemporary worship. I looked down on the simplistic lyrics of praise music, the extemporaneous prayers with their questionable theology and casual way of worship. I looked down on its theology and on the people who loved singing its songs and praying its prayers. Compared with a noble hymn like "The Church's One Foundation," a song like "Shout to the Lord" seemed to me to be simplistic, cheap, and intellectually empty.

While I served at a cathedral church, I was proud of its tasteful worship and music, its dignified way of doing liturgy. I loved the intellectually stimulating sermons, the dignified prayers, and the grand language of worship that has been part of the Church for centuries. It was a feast for all the senses.

And then I went to a memorial service at the Salvation Army for one of its members. Bill used to come every week to the cathedral's evening prayer service for the poor and homeless. In true Anglican style, though we made the worship more casual, we had printed programs, written prayers with congregational responses, and a short sermon. We would see Bill, tall and dignified, walking very slowly up the slope to the chapel with his cane and his gentle smile. A retired teacher, he was bright and friendly. He always sat in the front row. One time, we asked him to lead one of the services, and he was inspiring to all of us.

When Bill died, I finally went to his church for the memorial service at the Salvation Army chapel downtown. As I sat there, I gritted my teeth. The room was plain, the talks were trite, the music was bad, and the theology was appalling. Then, after I left, I wondered: Was I just invited to Bill's feast, and I turned it down? If this was his church, he was much more tolerant and gracious about our formal worship than I was of his casual and heartfelt one.

Contemporary worship, in all its forms—folk, evangelical, young, different—seeks out the longings of people where they are, and nourishes their longings. Not everybody is fed by nineteenth-century English choral music. For some people, traditional worship "has nothing to do with me" and so fails to touch their spirit or their heart.

I am ashamed of my elitist attitude. Contemporary worship, or informal services, or any worship service that does not meet my intellectual and sensory standards is not bad taste. Maybe I am the one with the bad taste—the taste of worship arrogance.

3 Lent: Wednesday

God Waits in Line

Recently I slipped on an icy pavement and landed on my head. When I came to, I got up, took care of three worship services and a class, met a friend, and then was taken to the emergency room. Then I prayed, giving thanks to God for being alive.

Later I realized that I had gotten the order all wrong.

Somehow, God ended up being last on my bureaucratic order of daily life. That doesn't always happen. When I wake up in the morning, the first thing I do is thank God—for the coming day, for my family and my cats, for my work and ministry, for my soft and comfortable pillow.

But sometimes, God gets lost in my bureaucracy. Why? I would never neglect to feed my cats, or wash the dishes, or turn off lights and lock my doors at night. I don't neglect the daily prayers that are part of my routine life.

Perhaps that's the problem. When I confine most of my conversations with God to daily morning and evening prayer, I separate God from the rest of my day—my frustrations, fumblings, and even accidents. I don't mean to separate God. But when prayer is part of my bureaucratic order of life, prayer itself can become bureaucratic.

Sometimes, like any bureaucracy, our brain goes on autopilot. It's hard to pay close attention all of the time, even in prayer. I remember one Sunday, during the Eucharistic Prayer, the congregational response came out of my mouth as "We remember his death, we proclaim his resurrection, we await his coming in Kroger." He will come to Kroger grocery store, I'm sure, but in our proclamation, we await his coming in glory.

Paul told us to "pray without ceasing." When my everyday activity is infused with a running conversation with God, when God is woven into the fabric of my ordinary times, the whole concept of prayer stops looking like an administrative chore and starts feeling like a relationship with the Beloved. And then, the next time I find myself lying on the ground, I might first call God, and then 911. God will always be there, even before the ambulance.

3 Lent: Thursday

Prayer too Deep for Words

Perseverance in Prayer
LUKE 11:9-13

Would God ever mistake a snake for a fish, or a scorpion for an egg, and give us the wrong thing? Doesn't God give us good gifts, just as imperfect parents give us good gifts, when we ask?

We assume that we know what's best for us. We assume that we ask for what's best for us. When we care for those around us, we look at their situations and often think we know how to pray for their best interests as well.

Of course a parent would not give us a scorpion if we ask for an egg. That may be the wrong scenario. It is more likely that, with a child's innocence, we might naively ask God for a scorpion, thinking we are asking for an egg.

We grow up learning to discern our needs and to distinguish what we want from what we need. When my daughter was young, I let her pack her own suitcase for a family trip. When she finished, I looked into the suitcase. It contained two pair of socks, two dolls, a bunch of doll clothes, and a hairbrush. That's what she thought she would need for the trip. We may pack comparable suitcases for our spiritual journeys.

When we are young, we pray for good grades, good friends, or a nice day at school. We pray for success and for results. As we get older, we learn to pray that our children will be happy or that we find a better job. But in God's eyes, that "better job" may be more like a scorpion, more harmful than enriching to our spiritual life. A child may need to go through a personal wilderness that pains me to see, and then she may emerge stronger and more enriched than my own small prayer would allow.

It may be that our best prayer is a request "too deep for words," trusting God to take us step-by-step to what is best for us and for our loved ones. Sometimes the best prayer is this one taken from *The Book of Common Prayer* (p. 831):

Almighty God, we entrust all who are dear to us to your never-failing care and love, for this life and the life to come, knowing that you are doing for them better things than we can desire or pray for; through Jesus Christ our Lord. *Amen.*

3 Lent: Friday

The Surrender of Plan A

Father, if it is possible, let this cup pass from me;
yet not what I want but what you want.
MATTHEW 26:39

My plan was simple. I was going to work part-time while raising my children, and in my free time, I would volunteer at their school. I was sure God would approve. It was sensible, fulfilling, and faithful. I saw no better way to live. As it turned out, though, the whole plan fell apart, and it was clear that God called me to a new life of teaching and preaching. Later, it turned out, the path to ordained ministry, which I had resisted taking, ended up being the best thing for me, and the most sensible and faithful.

We all have our Plan A, both big and little. I plan how big my family will be and how I will graduate and find the right job. I have a plan for how I will pay back the money I borrowed from my brother Randy by making a little extra cash selling my collection of baseball bobbleheads on the side.

Sometimes Plan A is more of an anti-plan. For Lent, I'll never give up chocolate. I'll never live in the Midwest, or the South, or the suburbs, or where I grew up. I'll never raise children or cats. I'll never, never be able to teach or speak out loud in public. That's often when God, in some perversely droll way, makes it clear that what we say never to is exactly what we are told to do. And it will be surprisingly right for us.

Plan A is my plan. We often talk about a Plan A and a Plan B, trying to anticipate and to control the direction of our lives. But what about God's plan? Is my plan for me the same as God's plan for me? If not, am I willing to give up my plan in order to follow God's?

Sometimes, God's plan takes us on a much more difficult path than our own plan for ourselves. God's path is sometimes more arduous, more vulnerable, and more challenging than we would want. So it is hard to surrender to God's plan.

Jesus knew that. On the night of his betrayal, he went into the garden and prayed to God, "Father, if it is possible, let this cup pass from me; yet not what I want but what you want" (Matthew 26:39). Staring into the cup and seeing in its reflection his own brutal death, he renounces his desire to avoid that future.

Jesus' act of surrender to God's will is incomprehensible to most of us, given what God's will was for him. But when Jesus prayed to God, he said in effect, "God's plan isn't even close to my Plan A or even Plan B for me, and I recoil from it—but I accept your desire for me, however incomprehensible it may seem to me right now." Jesus' powerful act of submission to God shows a deep trust that comes only with a strong faith, not by being sure but by being vulnerable—vulnerable to God. That's so much more fulfilling than any Plan A that I could ever concoct.

3 Lent: Saturday

Sabbath as Sacrament

S is for sabbath, or Sunday.

Sometimes I wish that S is for Snooze alarm, or Sleep. S is for Snuggling with my cat, for Saying No to the call of the computer or the call of the office.

Some have said that when we observe a sabbath time of rest, we are saying "no" to a culture of work. That is true. But sabbath rest should be more than a negative message to ourselves and to the world.

When we are pressured to work every day, our time-out is a rebellion, an alternative to the hamster wheel of relentless productivity and economic efficiency.

But sabbath at its best is a time of saying "yes." It's a time to say yes to God, yes to entering the holy creation, yes to recreation— that is, to re-creation. When we give ourselves time to take a holy breath, we allow ourselves to become part of God's new Creation. We allow ourselves to enter into an earthly model of the heavenly city, where sabbath is the norm, not the alternative. And we allow ourselves time with God—not just for a few minutes of prayer but as an integral part of at least one day.

Sabbath and prayer are intimately connected. Sabbath is a time of lived prayer. During the time we spend with God as our center, we offer ourselves sacramentally to God.

And then, just as in the sacrament of Holy Eucharist, the one presiding holds a spotlight to the holy, so in a sacrament of sabbath, we may be a spotlight to the divine, a spotlight to the love and goodness of God.

How will you live Sabbath tomorrow?

S is for sabbath, for Sunday, for spotlight, for sacrament. S is for saying yes to God.

Fourth Week in Lent

A Day in the Life of Jesus' Parables:
Being a Living Parable

4 Lent: Sunday

Stories for Grown-ups:
The Trouble with Parables

The trouble with Jesus' parables is that, if we take them seriously, they make us feel uncomfortable.

I used to find comfort and pride in Jesus' parables.

Am I not better than that arrogant and greedy rich man who would not share even the crumbs from his table with the poor man Lazarus? Unlike him, I will not end up in flaming eternity.

Am I not better than the two men who passed by the man beaten on the road on the way to Jericho? I would be the Good Samaritan who helps him up, bandages his wounds, and pays for his keep at the nearest hotel until he recovers.

The Parable of the Prodigal Son is trickier, because I am definitely not like the elder brother who gripes because his wayward brother is welcomed home as if he'd never left. But I am also definitely not like the prodigal son who takes his inheritance and squanders it on gambling and questionable nightclub living. But I could be like the son when he returns to his home, humbled and repentant.

I am definitely better than that Pharisee, who arrogantly thanks God that he is better than the wicked tax collector over in the corner. This makes me spiritually more like the tax collector, even though in practice I am more like the Pharisee—a good person who pays my taxes and gives to the church and practices my spiritual disciplines regularly.

At some point, it occurred to me that Jesus' parables make me feel uncomfortable because they are not congratulating me on how good I am. Some of the parables take a lot of mental contortions to put myself on the good guy's side. So they remind me more of how sinful I am, even as I congratulate myself. And in a most awkward moment of truth, Jesus reminds me that my own self-congratulation betrays me.

Jesus makes us sympathize with his saved characters, and so we identify with them. But more often, my truth lies with the indifference of the passersby, the snobbery of the elder brother, or the haughtiness of the Pharisee. How many times have I passed by a ragged man and refused to even look him in the eye? How many times have I resented special treatment for someone who doesn't deserve it? How many times have I thanked God that I'm not like that ill-mannered woman or the dirty man next to me on the bus with the greasy boots and the mumbling talk?

I am the wrong character. I am the rich man. I am the priest and the Levite, and I am the Pharisee.

But there is hope. I can learn from the tax collector who says, "God, be merciful to me, a sinner!"

4 Lent: Monday

The Temp Worker

The Laborers in the Vineyard
MATTHEW 20:1-16

She has gone to the employment center every morning for two years, looking for work. She arrives very early, at 4:30 a.m., so that she might have a better chance. Sometimes she is hired, but sometimes there is no work for her that day.

She sits on the folding chair as others are called by name. Those who are called climb into the rickety school bus and head out to the tech company or the packing company, where they will work all day—for one day. These men and women will be back tomorrow to do it again.

The woman, though, is not called. She sits and waits while a second batch of names is called, to be transported to other places. By mid-morning, she still sits. She wants to work, but no one wants her. She depends on work to feed her two sons and to pay rent on her single room at the boarding house. She can't find a regular job, so she comes here. It is her only chance.

Finally, her name is called. It is past noon. She will only work two hours, so she will only get a quarter-day's pay—ten dollars, and from that, they will deduct a fee for transportation on the bus. That's barely enough for even a day's food for her family, but she is grateful for the work anyway. What she will do if she gets sick, she doesn't know.

When the work is over, all of the temporary workers line up for their day's pay. The ones who came first are eager to go home, so they are first in line. When the supervisor gives them their wages, in cash, he counts the money out loud: "Ten, twenty, thirty, forty dollars. There you are." Then he hands it to the first temp worker who pockets the money as the supervisor moves on down the line. "Ten, twenty, thirty, forty."

When he gets to the last person, the woman, he counts out, "Ten, twenty, thirty, forty bucks. There you are." And he hands her the bills. Her eyes open wide. She has received the pay for a full day's work. Her heart quivers with joy as she thanks him politely.

The supervisor smiles when he hears the grumbling from the other workers, the ones who came to work earlier. Today, every single worker will go home and enjoy a full meal with their families, at least for today. "Thank you, God," he says to himself. "Thank you for letting me help this woman's family eat."

4 Lent: Tuesday

The Neo-Nazi

The Good Samaritan
LUKE 10:25-37

David came to church for the weekly dinner. He was big and intimidating and wore a camouflage vest. Actually, it was a jacket so old that the sleeves were gone. Maybe they were torn off from a fight. He also wore a Mohawk haircut. Like I said, he was intimidating. He boasted that he was a neo-Nazi. Once I asked him why he was homeless. "Because I choose to be," he answered, without smiling.

The downtown church fed the poor and homeless every week, and he was a regular. But it was a stretch for him, because many of the guests were African American. He would sit quietly at the round table, not speaking much to anyone, but he liked the meals. And he was always polite.

Dwayne also came to dinner regularly. One evening just after dinner, Dwayne suddenly collapsed on the street down the block from the church. Poor, African American, with kidney problems, maybe he looked like a stereotypical drunk man lying on the street. As he curled up on the street in pain, no one stopped to help. Businessmen walked by, wanting to get home to their families. Families passed by on their way to the baseball game. Probably everybody assumed that somebody else would help this man.

Then David the neo-Nazi guy came out of the church and saw Dwayne the African American. He ran back inside and called for somebody to call 911. Then he ran back outside, knelt by Dwayne, took off his jacket and placed it under Dwayne's head for a pillow. He stayed with Dwayne until the ambulance came.

The next week, David came to dinner and brought a blanket for Dwayne to use, because with his medical problems, he often got shivers. As for Dwayne, he also came to dinner. He brought with him a new XXXL camouflage jacket for David because it was getting cold, and David could use a jacket with sleeves. And they sat together at dinner—two guests at the Lord's table.

4 Lent: Wednesday

The Model Citizen

The Pharisee and the tax collector
LUKE 18:9-14

Then afterward I will pour out my spirit on all flesh;
your sons and your daughters shall prophesy, your old men
shall dream dreams, and your young men shall see visions.
Even on the male and female slaves, in those days, I will
pour out my spirit.
JOEL 2:28-29

In the world of business, school, and other places, it makes sense to add up your achievements and measure yourself against other people. That's how we get good grades or good jobs. That's how we get ahead in this world. I deserve a better position in my company because I am a better worker. At least I don't fall asleep at my desk like Mr. Tax Collector over there. Thank you, God, that I'm not like my coworker, who cheats on his time card. We measure ourselves against each other all the time, in big and little ways.

But as soon as we go out of the world of business and into the world of God—which the Pharisee does as soon as he enters the temple to pray—it's a different measurement. It's not about getting ahead or being better than everybody else. Everybody's a sinner. Everybody gets the sun on his or her back, everybody gets rained on—the good and the bad, rich and poor, saints and sinners, Pharisees and tax collectors.

And Mr. Pharisee was one of the saints—one of the good guys. The Pharisee is the one we really do look up to. He's a model citizen. He worships regularly, and he even tithes!

The funny thing is that the Pharisee nowadays has the same bad reputation as the tax collector in those days. Mr. Pharisee says, "Thank you, God, that I'm not like that awful tax collector." But today, if you call somebody a Pharisee, that's an insult. "You—you Pharisee!" That can make somebody cry. It's like calling somebody a grouchy, conceited hypocrite. Nowadays we say, or think, "Thank God, I'm not like a Pharisee."

Luke says that Mr. Pharisee will go home feeling exalted but eventually will be humbled, while Mr. Tax Collector will go home feeling humbled but eventually will be exalted. But I believe they will both end up on the same level plain, in the kingdom. For God promises to pour out the sun, the rain, and the Holy Spirit upon all flesh, including Pharisee flesh and tax collector flesh.

God promises the Holy Spirit to all those who have ever done wrong, or made mistakes, or failed in geometry, or cheated on their taxes, or been arrogant like the Pharisee.

God promises the Holy Spirit to all those who are good, who think they are doing right, and who try to do right but can never live up to the standards of perfection.

God promises to us all God's spirit of love, compassion, and mercy. There's plenty to go around, and God is generous. That should make all of us tax collectors happy, and it should give all of us Pharisees pause.

4 Lent: Thursday

Deborah and Barbie

The Weeds Among the Wheat
MATTHEW 13:24-30

When I met Richard and Deborah, they told me they had just been reunited. "How long were you apart?" I asked. Richard said, "Seventeen years. I was in prison for seventeen years." Deborah had waited for him all that time, a faithful wife. "And God was with me, too," he adds.

Now they are homeless. With his criminal record, even though he did not drink or do drugs, he could not find a job. And without a job, he has no money for rent. He shows me a photo that someone had taken of them, on the corner of Third and Vine. "This is our living room," he jokes.

Living in the middle of the business district, in a way, Richard and Deborah are weeds among wheat. People are embarrassed by the presence of this dirty, disheveled couple spreading their blankets on the corner bench on a major city street. They cart their belongings around on a Radio Flyer wagon—mostly blankets, cardboard boxes laid flat to serve as mattresses, and a few pieces of clothing.

Richard and Deborah come to dinner every week. I notice that Deborah wears only a denim jacket as her outerwear, even when it's really cold outside. Barbie has a much bigger wardrobe than Deborah has, I think suddenly.

When my daughter was young, I bought countless elegant outfits for her Barbie dolls. In total, the cost of these doll clothes probably exceeded Deborah's net worth by thousands of dollars. We live in a society where a doll's budget might be higher than some people's wages, and we spend more money on toys than some people earn in a year.

I went out and bought a new puffy coat for Deborah, so she could stay warm while sleeping outside. But I never saw her wear it. I suspect that she sold it for food. Once you're behind, it's so hard to keep up with Barbie.

It took two years, but Richard and Deborah finally found a place to live, thanks to a sympathetic benefactor who saw him and took hope in his determination to survive. The benefactor paid for schooling for Richard, then helped him to find a job. And now they both volunteer to help others who are homeless. Through all those years, Deborah stayed with him. They were thought to be weeds, but they refused to be pulled out and thrown away, and they have turned out to be wheat—productive and valuable in the community. God always knew that.

4 Lent: Friday

Workers and Worry Dolls

Do Not Worry
MATTHEW 6:25-34

They say the American middle class is disappearing, being replaced by a tiny wealthy few and a huge pool of people who are poor or lower class because of shrinking incomes, overwhelming debt, lower wages, and a decline in middle-income jobs. Some say they can never retire, others have seen their retirement savings shredded. When I am retired, or laid off, or out of money, what will I eat? What will I wear? Will I end up sleeping under a bridge? Am I of such little value in this world?

Meanwhile, Jesus tells us, "Do not worry about your life, what you will eat or what you will drink, or about your body, what you will wear…Strive first for the kingdom of God and his righteousness, and all these things will be given to you as well."

In a simplistic rendering of this advice, one would buy a supply of worry dolls, those tiny woven dolls that you can hold in your hand dozens at a time. According to Guatemalan tradition, if you cannot sleep at night, speak your worries to your worry doll and then place it under your pillow when you go to sleep. The doll will then do your worrying for you, and you can sleep peacefully and wake up rested, your worries all gone. The worry dolls are very popular with children, but I doubt that most adults would find much help in them.

Is Jesus turning God into a worry doll? In this era of economic uncertainty, how can we heed Jesus' advice not to worry? How can we merely "strive for the kingdom of God" and then expect that we will be clothed and fed?

God does not control layoffs, foreclosures, or medical bills. God does not guarantee steady work, a sustainable wage for workers, fair and just working conditions, or a stock market that will help us to retire comfortably. These are very real anxieties, and it would be wrong to spiritualize these very real stresses. God knows we need food, drink, clothing and shelter, just as birds need food and lilies need rain.

We don't know the context of Jesus' advice—who his hearers are, what they are worried about or why. But we know about God, and so did Jesus. Jesus tells us again and again that God is with us when we struggle. He reassures us that God cares about us, just as, or even more than, God cares for the marvelous birds of the air and the gorgeous lilies of the field. His reassuring message is the verbal equivalent of a comforting hug. Unlike a worry doll, God will not only hear our worries but also will walk with us through our troubles.

I don't think Jesus will condemn us if we worry about how to survive in our tough economic times. But certainly today we might find comfort knowing how much God values us, even when we question it ourselves.

4 Lent: Saturday

The Song of the Wedding Feast

The Great Dinner
LUKE 14:15-24

The Wedding Banquet
MATTHEW 22:1-10

The king plans a wedding feast for his son. He throws open the palace doors to all, no matter their station in life, no matter whether they are good or bad, no matter whether they are rich, poor, arrogant, humble, native or foreign, or even makeing excuses for not coming at first. Eventually they will all come and occupy the palace with the best seats in the house.

God promises a feast. What is the nature of the feast for us? Think about the metaphor of food. If it's your feast, depending on your heritage, a feast may be what you have grown up to love. A feast may be a meal of deep-fried pickles, goetta sandwiches, and sauerkraut balls. Or it may be coq au vin and sweetbreads in cream sauce. For me, it may be bird's nest soup, Peking duck, and mustard greens in soy sauce. Our differing ideas of feast tell me that, if anything, the party will be an open house. It won't be just my feast or my heaven, with my food and my friends.

And the feast that awaits us, when all people flock to it, may be not one prepared *by* the Lord, but one prepared in joy and thanksgiving *for* the Lord. What if heaven is like a giant potluck for our God and for one another? Maybe heaven is where we make a feast for the Lord, and the feast is not so much an abundance of things but an abundance of community.

Now there's a feast. At the table with me are all the people we've met this week: the model citizen, the temp worker, the neo-Nazi, the worried worker, the poor, the sick, the rich, the humble, and even the arrogant.

This is the wedding feast of the Lord—an occasion to restore communion with each other, to restore public trust, and to uphold life and prosperity for all with an attitude of respect and appreciation for all people. This happens only when we share our feast—which is to say, when we share earth and the abundant resources that God has given us. The kingdom of heaven will come with the just, righteous, and holy sharing of our feast—a kind of Occupy Earth.

Let the hope for a just society occupy our prayers, occupy our neighborhood, and occupy our churches.

Fifth Week in Lent

God's Compassionate Community

5 Lent: Sunday

A Grown-Up Faith:
Holy Connections to a Holy Life

Scientists, looking for planets orbiting other suns, just found an earth-sized planet orbiting in a star's "Goldilocks" zone—not too hot, not too cold, but "just right" for possible life.

If there are as many as a billion stars in the many billions of galaxies, it's becoming easier to imagine that there are many billions of living beings that God has created and holds in the palm of God's hand. We don't know what they look like or how they would live—and we wonder whether they, too, sin against God and need to be forgiven and redeemed like we do.

The possibility of life elsewhere always raises the worry that we on earth are not the center of the universe. We found out a long time ago that the earth is not the center, and then that the sun is not the center, and then that our galaxy is not the center. But to realize that we humans are not the center of God's universe is both comforting (we are not alone!) and scary (we are not the only beloveds!).

But we don't need to go into deep space to know that we are not the only beloveds of God's creation. We just need to look down on the ground, in the sky, in the earth, or in the waters. Because the giant octopuses are not human, does God love them less? Is the anteater not also a beloved creature of God? Has the mosquito not also been brought into being by a loving God?

We do not know how God speaks to other creatures. But we should be wary of assuming that because other creatures are not like us, they do not matter to God. They too are holy life, as we are. They too are a vital part of this earth. We humans are not alone in this universe, and we are not the only beloveds.

But that does not diminish us. Rather, we may be proud and honored to be part of a community of holy life. The multitudes of life nourish and sustain us, and we are called by God to nourish and sustain them. That is the beloved community that God desires for all of God's creatures, anteaters and humans alike.

5 Lent: Monday

Poor Stewart

Blind Bartimaeus
MARK 10:46-52

I buried one of my cats recently. Poor Stewart. He was a sweet-looking rescue cat, but he had issues. He was an obese, bulimic cat with stress-induced asthma. Every time we talked about him, we would say, "poor Stewart." But I don't think that Stewart thought of himself as "poor Stewart." You would think that with his medical problems, Stewart would be a nasty sort, the kind that would kick anybody in his way. But Stewart was gentle and sweet, despite the raw deal that genetics and nature dealt to him. We labeled him "poor Stewart," but that wasn't the real Stewart. The real Stewart should have been called "sweet Stewart."

We do this a lot. There is a man whom Jesus healed that we call Blind Bartimaeus. The funny thing is, though we know him for all time as Blind Bartimaeus, it seems that he was not always blind. He asks Jesus, "My teacher, let me see again." So it seems that he once had his eyesight. Somehow during his life—and it may have been only last year; who knows?—he lost his sight and has been reduced to begging because he can't make a living all by himself. His own community deserted him the moment he became disabled. So when he sees Jesus, he is blind. And when Jesus restores his sight, he can see. We still label him as Blind Bartimaeus, as if that is all he was, is, and ever shall be. But in fact, that's not the real Bartimaeus. The real Bartimaeus has a real name and has been exiled to the streets because he happens to be blind. When Jesus heals him, he not only restores his eyesight— he restores his community to him, so Bartimaeus can be his true self rather than his poor self or his blind self.

What Jesus knows, and what we still need to learn, is that our true humanity is lived out in community. We are meant to live in communion with each other, not in isolation. That's why ostracism or exile is such a devastating punishment. A community that makes a practice of labeling people like Blind Bartimaeus and then banishing them because of their blindness is a broken community.

So I wonder: Who are the Blind Bartimaeuses now? Where are the places of exile to which we send them? How do we label people in order to keep them forever in their place? Blind Bart? Poor Stewart? Homeless Harry? Sex Offender Travis? How do these labels that we assign to people shape our communities?

I notice that I label people a lot—and I put myself in a ladder of ascending and descending categories of worth and value. These categories contain my uncharitable thoughts and false judgments toward others, but I fit myself into one of the better boxes. Where do I fit in? What box do others put me in?

It is time for us to give up our labels. Because in our labeling, we put all the Blind Bartimaeuses out in the streets. We diminish their humanity and devalue their worth. Does homeless equal worthless? Unemployed equal lazy? Ethnic equal inferior or quaint? Blind equal banished?

With labels such as these, we place whole cohorts of people into the badlands of poverty and hopelessness. Whether or not

Bartimaeus became blind by accident or birth, he was exiled not by God, rather by his community and by the norms that excluded him and counted him as worthless. But Jesus shows us another way—a compassionate, merciful, and divine way to be the community of the beloved. In this community, we give up our labeling compulsion and embrace a community in which all people, blind or not, white or African American or Muslim or purple, are brought together in peace and respect, in wholeness and healing.

5 Lent: Tuesday

Investing with God

The Parable of the Talents
MATTHEW 25:14-30

"Aach! You should have invested my money with the bankers, and I would have gotten back everything I gave you, plus interest! What a bad person you are!"

Actually, these days, I wonder whether the third servant didn't make the best choice by stashing his employer's money away instead of investing it in a bank funded by mortgage-backed securities. The poor servant was just being prudent, and what's wrong with that? Why does Jesus scold someone who was cautious about investing their boss's money? But Jesus is not giving us financial advice. And he's no Dear Abby either, handing out advice about taking risks or being courageous. Jesus is telling us about the kingdom of God and what to do with its wealth. God's wealth is different, because God's economy is extravagant, based on the attitude of abundance. God gives us an infinite gift of grace, love, and forgiveness that never runs out.

Who are we to hoard God's abundance of wealth or to put a lid on it? But we often do. Like that prudent servant, we keep it hidden, crammed under mattresses or tucked deep into our hearts. No one can find it beneath our defenses, our cynicism, our various resentments, our comforts, and our conceits. In other words, what God so freely gives, we hoard and hide.

But Jesus warns us not to take abundance and turn it into scarcity. If we believe in scarcity, we will live by scarcity's rules, always hoarding and holding on and defending ourselves, afraid that, like our worldly goods, God's riches might run out. However, if we are willing to try to live trusting in God's abundance, in that economy of grace, we can freely share as God freely gives.

In Appalachia and in other parts of the country with abundant natural resources, businesses in the past have taken the abundance of the earth and turned it into scarcity, by exploiting the land and the people. Mountaintop removal and the clearcutting of forests destroys the land; low wages and dangerous working conditions endanger the workers. We are learning that abundance for all means abundance for each of us, and that exploiting and degrading any of us exploits and degrades us all. We are learning to practice sustainable development of our natural resources. Abundance for me does not have to mean scarcity for somebody else. We are beginning to remember a faraway Eden, in which we embrace our connectedness to and our dependence on one another, and where all people have the full and overflowing measure of what they need.

God gives us an abundance of gifts—grace and truth, the Holy Spirit, joy and wonder in creation, hearts to love and the strength to persevere. We must not turn these gifts into scarcity by hoarding or putting a lid over them. When we see someone in need and are "tempted" (as we so bizarrely say) to give generously, we are called to remember that God's abundance is not bound by the limits of human scarcity. When we give to one, we give to ourselves, and we give to God, and the whole kingdom grows. When we feed someone who is hungry, we feed ourselves, and we feed the King, and the whole kingdom grows.

We might want to hide our money under a mattress these days, so the money doesn't get used up. But don't hide God's love under that mattress. Don't mistake God's unlimited abundance for the finite riches of this world. God's love and mercy will never, never run out.

5 Lent: Wednesday

Distressed Properties

The Two Foundations
LUKE 6:47-49

The housing crisis that happened several years ago was part of a far-reaching economic crisis that taught us painful lessons. From this situation, we learned a whole new vocabulary—subprime mortgages, short sales, foreclosures, credit default swaps, predatory lending. We learned much about corporate financial recklessness, and how that affects all of us.

One of the more fascinating new concepts that I have learned from the real estate world is the concept of "distressed property." This refers to a home that is being separated from its owner—a home that is losing its owner because he or she can no longer pay the mortgage, and the property is being foreclosed. Often the home is abandoned by the time foreclosure takes place.

Two things often happen with distressed properties. First, the value of the property goes down; it is deemed to be worth less than the properties around it. Second, the place, especially when it has been abandoned, suffers physical deterioration; it is uncared for. I find it interesting to hear about a "distressed property"—interesting and sad, because it makes vivid what I suppose to be the feelings of the owners more than the situation of the house.

When times are tough, people feel a little like a distressed property. In an unstable and uncertain world, we sometimes feel as if we are losing our anchor—losing our owner, so to speak. We may feel unvalued or uncared for. We may be treated by others as unworthy. We may even feel abandoned.

Jesus tells us to build our lives on the solid rock—the rock of the kingdom of God. But the solid rock on which our souls can stand is not our own righteousness. The rock is God's love for us and God's assurance that our salvation has nothing to do with our purity or our worthiness, and everything to do with God's forgiving love. When we build our house on solid rock—our lives on God's love—we know God will never treat us like distressed properties. We are of infinite value to God, and we can be sure that God will never abandon us.

5 Lent: Thursday

Blessed Are the Truckers

I never paid much attention to the big trucks until I began commuting to work on a major interstate. Then it occurred to me that the interstates belong to the trucks. At first, I looked down on those big semis, the eighteen wheelers. They were a nuisance. They moved too slowly, they took up too much of the road, and they blocked my view of the road signs. Once, as I passed a slow-moving truck, I also passed my exit, ending up miles away from my destination. Trucks were irritating.

One snowy Midwest winter, a huge multi-car accident made the news. The newscaster noted most cars had been driving too fast and were unable to stop when they saw the pile-up ahead of them. But not a single big truck crashed because the drivers, according to the reporter, were "the professionals."

I had never thought of truck drivers as the professionals before. In fact, I had never even thought of them at all. I have only seen the trucks and thought of them as moving obstacles that annoyed me. The drivers were invisible to me, just like the contents that they carried. But the big trucks make so many things readily available to us—our food, cars, clothes—and almost everything else we need for daily life. Until I heard somebody talk about truck drivers as the road professionals who normally drive slowly and steadily in order to be safer than the harried and hurried commuters, I never made the connection between those trucks, my own lifestyle, and our common life. I had not respected the people who drive those trucks and make my lifestyle possible. In anthropomorphizing the trucks by seeing them as irritating bullies, I dehumanized the drivers.

This happens a lot. When I go to the store, the people ahead of me in the checkout line are merely obstacles to my ability to get home faster. I do not really see their faces. I don't stop to realize the woman in front of me also wants to get home. I don't appreciate that she has just finished working her second job and wants to be with her son, who has been home alone because she can't afford childcare. I only see her grocery cart filled with ten times more items than I have. When my garbage cans are emptied, I don't think about the men who lift the heavy, dirty cans and lug them to the truck, house after house, block after block, day after day. I just get irritated when their truck blocks my car, or when they leave the garbage can lid open and rain falls into the can.

But we are part of a larger whole, interconnected and interdependent. One of the prayers at Compline puts things like this: "our common life depends on each other's toil" (*The Book of Common Prayer*, p. 134). The kingdom of God is a holy community in which we honor all persons. With a grown-up faith, we see the face of God in each person. And we become the face of God to those whom we meet, especially those in need. With a grown-up faith, the world becomes much more interesting, and we realize how deeply we are all connected to one another and to God.

Who are the people around me and how do I depend on them? What do the human faces of the truckers really look like? Do I honor them and their work, as they play their part in creating a sustainable world for all of us? Do I see in them the image of God, and in their work the work of God's kingdom?

Blessed be the truckers and all those who work for our common life. And blessed be the grown-up world of a grown-up faith, where we are all connected one to another and to God in God's beloved community.

5 Lent: Friday

The Odds of Healing

Jairus' Daughter and the Woman Who Touched Jesus' Cloak
MARK 5:21-43

My parents tried their luck with slot machines very occasionally. Once my whole family went to Reno for the weekend, and my parents didn't have much luck at the slots. As we were just leaving the motel to go home, a single slot machine stood by the exit door. One more chance. Mom and Dad both used up all their money, so they turned to me and my siblings for help, and one of us managed to dig up a single quarter. Dad put it into the machine—nothing came out. The odds were against him. What were the odds of winning, anyway?

I think of the gambling odds when I hear the stories of Jesus healing a woman suffering from continual bleeding after twelve years, or the girl who died, ready to be brought to life just when Jesus shows up. What are the odds? It must have been like winning the jackpot for both of these women!

Jesus drew crowds wherever he went—major league baseball crowds and rock concert crowds. Of those people, two people are healed. Why them? If Jesus wants to heal, why does he just heal one at a time? If the point was for Jesus to heal people, his ministry might be classified as a failure, or at least a bad strategy on his part. If he loved Capernaum so much, why didn't he just walk to the top of the hill and heal the whole town?

But Jesus healing a person—or even all the people—is not the point. Healing is not even the point. If we believe that our life, and our health, and our physical bodies are the point, then being healed by Jesus is like winning the jackpot at the Casino Divina, because the odds are against us. When I see myself in the crowd, I want to win the jackpot and be the recipient of God's healing.

And that's why winning the Casino Divina jackpot is a deceptive, illusory hope. When we think that if we have enough faith we will be healed, or if we pray enough we will be healed, then healing is like winning the jackpot. Some will win, but most won't. When we look more intently at the big picture, and realize it's not about us but about God, then we can answer the question, "What's going on with Jesus' healing, anyway?"

Jesus' healing works are not about the works themselves. Jesus is turning a spotlight to God beyond. He is not showing us what healing is about, but what God is about. By paying attention to a marginalized woman and making her whole again, he gives us a living parable about the abundant, profligate, indiscriminate power of God to make whole a broken person and a broken world. There is hope even for someone as hopeless as a twelve-year-old dead girl, because God's all-embracing power reaches even beyond the grave.

That's good news for us—because everybody is an outcast with an incurable disease. The disease is called sin, and we all suffer from it. But Jesus points the way to what the kingdom is really about. Rather than Casino Divina, the kingdom is the triumph of God's powerful healing presence, the extravagant economy of grace and mercy poured into our broken and dying selves and world. Now that's a real jackpot!

5 Lent: Saturday

God on Wall Street

The Parable of the Dishonest Manager
LUKE 16:1-13

The story commonly known as the "Parable of the Dishonest Manager" is puzzling to many of us. When we hear the story, we usually take God to be the rich man who fires this clever fellow for spending too much of his employer's money and squandering his boss's property. In Jesus' parables, God is always the boss. In this story, the boss isn't looking so good. The boss looks unimaginative, or a little slow. And then, why would the boss praise the fired manager for squandering his property even more by reducing his clients' bills? God is in this story, but in a more subtle, deeper way. This is a parable for grownups, for today's post-modern, sometimes-cynical world. Here's how the parable might speak to us.

God is fired from Wall Street for being too easy on customers and recklessly spending the company's assets. The company runs in a very business-like but ethically challenged way. They overcharge their customers and give special deals to their rich clients. They charge more interest to the poor and give favorable treatment to the rich. They write misleading press releases about their stock, and they practice insider trading. The company is profitable and able to increase its assets and properties, but one of the business managers, God, gives better deals to the less wealthy, decreasing the company's profits. So the company fires God, claiming that God has squandered its assets.

So, God goes to Main Street, dressed in a business suit, and God does what God does. God forgives debts. It turns out that this act of settling accounts by refinancing loans draws clients into a better relationship with the marketplace. God's business model makes the business richer, not in assets but in customer relations. A dishonest manager? No, just one with a different ethic, a developed and compassionate ethic that works for the common good rather than self-interest.

God is shrewd. But God's success is about more than shrewd business practice; this is the only way that really works if we want a community of goodwill. Even when the business is wealth and possessions, money must not be the ruler. Money isn't inherently evil, but an obsession with possessing more material wealth can sabotage human relationships by placing money above people and productivity above compassion. With God, it's not about stuff, it's about the common good.

That raises up all of us, no matter what street we live on.

Holy Week

Palm Sunday

Bare Faith

At last we come to Palm Sunday—in many ways, my favorite service of the church year.

Palm Sunday has everything—the pomp and stateliness of the procession, the flashy red hangings at the altar, the gathered assembly belting out "All Glory, Laud and Honor," the palms that we carry as we re-enact Jesus' triumphal entry into Jerusalem. We hold close the sense of expectation, hope, and longing—and suddenly all that changes. The exalted theme gives way precipitously to the story of Jesus' trial, condemnation, and crucifixion. The full name of the service—The Sunday of the Passion: Palm Sunday—reflects its dual nature. Jubilation is overtaken by suffering. A triumphal procession turns into a funeral parade.

I love Palm Sunday because it is pure church. There is not a shred of commercialism in Palm Sunday. Just as with Ash Wednesday, the consumer culture has managed to miss this marketing opportunity. We are spared our material culture's impulse to take advantage of every holiday to sell us something.

When I open the Sunday paper on that day, there are no ads proclaiming Holy Week Hardware Special! Palm Sunday Car Sale. Buy Holy Week Passion Jewelry for Your Loved One!

On Palm Sunday, we are not confronted with a Passion donkey bearing gifts to put under a decorated palm tree. There are no electronic dancing palm trees or chocolate passion candy.

Palm Sunday is the Church with its faith laid bare.

And what a faith it is! Against the human tendency to market its strengths and congratulate itself on its achievements, Christianity confesses Christ crucified. Gone is all boasting. Instead, as we follow our Lord Jesus' path toward his passion, death, and resurrection, we lay bare our weakness. During Holy Week, the Church drops to its knees before God, making herself vulnerable to the One who became vulnerable for each and every one of us. The victory of Christ's resurrection is the victory of weakness over power, and the victory of generous love over scarcity and self-preservation.

Holy Week gives us the chance to experience our faith laid bare. It is unadorned faith, with nothing to distract us from the self-giving love of the living God. No marketing offer in the world can beat that.

Monday in Holy Week

Lost

S in is that big, heavy thing that separates us from right relationship with God. Sin also makes a case for the existence of hell. Ironically, it's also something that we often cannot clearly define. When I get mad at somebody, is that a sin? What about when I do something I don't know is wrong, like accidentally hurting someone's feelings by not paying attention to him? When does a mistake become a sin? When does our path in life go from "being lost" to "committing evil in the sight of the Lord?" When you hear the stories about the lost sheep and the lost coin, from a sinner's point of view, it looks like we need to atone for being clueless like sheep, or brainless like coins. Somehow I don't think that cluelessness or stupidity are sins.

Maybe that's the problem with sin. I would rather admit to being clueless or dumb than admit to being sinful. I'll say, "That was a dumb thing to do," or "I didn't know better." I would rather not say, "I wronged you. I was sinful." I am reminded of the great theologian Meister Eckhart, a profound medieval scholar in the days of the Inquisition. His ideas did not always sit well with the authorities. At one point they charged him with heresy. A brave man, Eckhart responded by charging the inquisitors with stupidity, which he considered the greater sin.

There are indeed greater sins that can be counted as evil— collective sins shared by entire society and institutions. I am part of a society, and an act that seems clueless or brainless to me can multiply into a collective failure to be the kind of community that God calls us to be.

The German theologian Johann Baptist Metz grew up in a little town in Bavaria. When he was older, he learned that his hometown was just thirty miles from the camp where Dietrich Bonhoeffer was killed. He asked his mother, "Did you know about that camp?" He said that she always claimed that she didn't know, that most people in town ignored it, maybe wondering what happened behind the closed gates but never asking the moral questions. The imprisonment of Japanese citizens in America during World War II and the treatment of African Americans as second-class citizens are other disturbing examples of our society being unable or unwilling to take a moral stand against sin.

I wonder: what are the sins of our society today, collective faults that remove us from God? And how do I contribute to those faults? How am I one of those lost sheep or lost coins that upholds injustice or keeps silent against evil? Is one of the sins our unbridled economic self-interest, which turns its back on the common good in pursuit of individual wealth? Might it be our careless exploitation and waste of precious natural resources, which threaten future generations with scarcity of water, wood, minerals, clean air, and all those essential things we need to survive?

As we become aware of unjust practices and institutional sins, it is not acceptable to ignore these sins as if they have nothing to do with us. If we turn our backs on what we know to be wrong, then we are not merely lost. If we just go along, saying, "We didn't know," without asking the big moral questions, we have lost our moral compass but I am not only lost. I am sinful.

The good news is that God never gives up on bringing us back to creating the community that God wants. God always reminds us that we can recalibrate our moral compass and regain a righteous voice in our society. We can be for others the face, voice, and hands of the Good Shepherd to bring back the wandering sheep and to find the misplaced coins.

Tuesday in Holy Week

The Superpower of Faith

The Parable of the Mustard Seed
MATTHEW 13:31-35

"If you had faith the size of a sesame seed, you could order a tree around and it would do whatever you want!" Wow. Faith gives us superpowers.

I read that many people unconsciously believe they have a secret superpower: say, for instance, the ability to influence the outcome of a major sporting event. My son didn't know what that meant until I told him I was afraid to listen to the Cincinnati Reds baseball game on the radio because I knew that if I did, they would lose.

"If you have enough faith…" "If I only had faith…" Does faith really give us superpowers, enough to levitate trees and move mountains? I remember a Sunday School lesson about the power of prayer. A neighborhood group transformed a parking lot in the middle of a big city into a plot of land. They divided the land into a bunch of little plots and let the inner-city residents grow tomatoes. Then a Christian group had the idea that some of their folks would randomly select plots to pray over throughout the summer. At the end of the season, the lesson continued, the plots that had been prayed over had bigger tomatoes than the other plots.

What did we learn? If I pray hard enough, will I end up with the biggest tomatoes of all? If my tomato plant looks scraggly, does that mean that I didn't have enough faith, and God doesn't love me or my tomatoes? How big are the tomatoes in your garden? Are you worried about your tomato plant as if your salvation depends on it? That would be a scary thought. Does God really care how big our tomatoes are? Does God really want to give us the power to grow a giant tomato through faith?

On the face of it, tomato theology sounds a little silly. But it's not unusual. The Bible is full of what looks like tomato theology—stories in which God rewards the faithful with success. By faith, the Bible says, Abraham is promised his own land and a ton of descendants. Because he has faith, Abraham gets the biggest tomatoes.

We ascribe to tomato theology all the time, in a more subtle form. During the hurricane, my house was spared from flooding, because God was with me. God cured my cancer. God helped me keep my job even when my coworkers were laid off. The trouble with "God is on my side" thinking is that it doesn't look very kindly on those who aren't so fortunate. What about the one who lost her job because the bank failed? Does God not love her? Many of us have faith in God, and our basements still flood, our bodies still get sick, our stocks and pensions fall just as much as everybody else's.

So maybe it's time to let go of the tomato theology of childhood and explore the deeper dimension of faith. In our grown-up mind, we know that faith in God doesn't enable us to break the laws of physics and manipulate the universe by levitating trees, or by making the Reds win the pennant. So what kind of faith does Jesus ask of us?

God wants us to have a faith that trusts in God. We place ourselves in God's care and open ourselves to God's healing touch. When we trust in God's loving care for us, God gives us grace to grow like a seed into the fullness of life. A seed is meant to grow, to transform into a large and mature plant. It is the same with faith and trust. When we trust in God, we give ourselves over to God's transformational love, forgiveness, and mercy, and then we are strong. That is how we become strong in love and hope. Even if the Reds lose the game, and our tomatoes are only average.

Wednesday in Holy Week

Life as Sacrament

Take my life, and let it be consecrated, Lord, to thee.
HYMNAL 1982, #707

On the night before he is killed, Jesus institutes a new sacrament, the Eucharist, in the event that we know as the Last Supper. And by reenacting this sacrament "in remembrance of me," we are invited to be sacraments as well, to live a holy life in remembrance of Jesus.

I have never considered my life as a sacrament before, as an "outward and visible sign of an inward and spiritual grace" (*The Book of Common Prayer*, p. 857). Most of the time I would be a poor and shameful sacrament indeed. I get up, feed the cats, go to work, talk with colleagues, eat my meals, go to bed. Sometimes I may do more, like serve in a soup kitchen or comfort someone who is grieving. But sometimes I do less, like hold a grudge against my sister for snubbing me at the last party or say something sarcastic about somebody I don't like.

Living life as a sacrament, a spotlight to the love and goodness of God, would be a challenge to me. I would need to be more conscious of how I act. I would need to be more mindful and more sensitive to people I meet. If I did some of those things, I could be an outward and visible sign of an inward and spiritual grace—the face of God to the world.

As we move deeper through our spiritual journey, closer to restoring a right relationship with God, how can we be the face of God to the world? How can we share with the world the gifts—the grace—that God has given to us?

God has given to us the gift of creation—the gift of life. An outward or sacramental sign of this gift might be an act that affirms life. We can fast from eating food that has resulted from the taking of life, or we can grow a garden or offer daily prayers for healing for those who are sick or dying.

God has given to us the love of God in Christ. An outward sign of this gift acknowledges this love by offering compassion and welcome. Feed the poor. Teach a child to read. Be a compassionate listener to somebody who is lonely.

God has given the gift of mercy. God is always merciful and slow to anger, always faithful to us and forgiving, even when we sin. To be a visible sign of God's mercy, we might show mercy by reaching out to someone in need or crisis, or by advocating for peace in our home, community, and world.

Given our weaknesses, frailty, and capacity for sin, we may think it impossible to be a sacrament. God knows better. God has given us gifts of life, love, and mercy because God knows how profoundly these gifts can change us, open us up, and empower us to live sacramental lives. God entrusts these gifts to us, not to hoard but to share them. Let us see our lives as God sees them, as sacraments and as holy temples for God. As a sacramental vessel for God, we learn we are both dust and children of God, we will both die and be risen, and we are both broken and beloved.

Maundy Thursday

The Table of the Lord

When I got married, my Chinese wedding banquet celebrated our biracial union. It was a ten-course meal of the fanciest, tastiest, most exotic food the Chinese can offer their guests. The meal celebrates a new family, and the food symbolically wishes the guests a long life, prosperity, and good fortune. The dinner always begins with soup. When it was served, my new mother-in-law took a sip and turned to my Chinese father next to her. "This soup is delicious!" "What is it?" My father paused for a few seconds. "I'll tell you later." By the time the meal was over, she had forgotten to ask again about the soup, and we were saved from having to witness a sudden cultural divide. She would have recoiled at the notion of tasting fish stomach soup. Such a specialized dish was a concrete illustration of an invisible cultural wall that often divides us, even at celebrations like wedding banquets.

Jesus likes to tell stories about wedding banquets, which he turns into chaotic open houses for the whole neighborhood rather than the usual guest list. Jesus expands our notion of wedding banquets and banquet etiquette by introducing us to the table manners of the kingdom of God. At Jesus' wedding banquets, he expands boundaries so that the whole world is invited. He expands the boundaries of everything else, too—his choice of friends and disciples, his choice of dinner companions, and the people he chooses to heal.

Jesus doesn't just heal lepers. He heals the whole world, as if we were all lepers. He doesn't just forgive tax collectors. He forgives the whole world, even those who killed him, because we are all sinners. There were the people he hung around with and called his friends, as if we are all equal: tax collectors, sinners, women, the diseased, the lame, the blind, and the beggars. These are the people who often repel us, the same way in which fish stomach soup repels some while hot dogs might repel others.

There are much more important things to be repelled by than soup or hot dogs, tax collectors and beggars—there's bigotry and injustice and letting poor people starve in a land of plenty. Violence toward women and little girls, not paying people a living wage, and closing doors to people who just need a second chance. Spreading hateful untruths about Sikhs, Muslims, gays and lesbians, ex-offenders, homeless people, and anyone who is different from us.

When we have courage and trust in God and in the memory of what Jesus said and did, we share the redemptive message of Jesus Christ. God's world is so much bigger than ours, and it challenges us to see where we can break out of our old boundaries and let God's redemptive message through Jesus Christ reach those whom we have left out. Once we get used to it, that bigger world is so much more palatable than our little one. If you try my fish stomach soup, I'll taste your deep-fried pickles.

Good Friday

Checkmate

What just happened? How did this happen so quickly, this sudden disastrous turn of events, this collapse from order to chaos, this end to an adventure that promised us a Messiah, an end to our oppression, and a kingdom of our own? How did we slide so quickly from victory to death?

Things seemed to be going so smoothly. People were being healed. There were rumors of a messiah, one who would overthrow the oppressors and free us to be our true selves again, under our true ruler. There were some disagreements among us at first, and confusion, but then at the end, everyone got carried away with inflammatory extremist ideas, and here we are, staring at Jesus, watching him die.

But it wasn't really that sudden. There were signs. We just didn't pick up on the signs—the warnings—because the signs were about us, not about them. We just kept going, and then we crossed the line and couldn't go back. We always assumed we were the good guys. So then, how did I end up holding this hammer and these nails? How did we become the executioners instead of the liberators?

It's hard to say that "we" crucified Jesus. The popular hymn "Ah, Holy Jesus," though, says it outright: "Who was the guilty? Who brought this upon thee? Alas, my treason, Jesus, hath undone thee. 'Twas I, Lord Jesus, I it was denied thee: I crucified thee'" (*Hymnal 1982*, #158). Two thousand years later, it's hard to see how I am the crucifier of our Lord. Do I still deny him?

When I turn a blind eye to hungry people, or when I condone excessively punitive sentences for offenders, or when I go along with our culture's love of violence, I make an imperceptible slide down the road holding the nails and hammer. When I go along with values that I know are contrary to Jesus' message of love, mercy, and forgiveness, I choose to make a turn down the conventional path that tells me to conform to a moral code other than God's. I deny my Lord.

Jesus keeps telling us about a kingdom. But his kingdom is unlike any other. It isn't a kingdom focused on power or any of power's benefits like wealth or domination, or even being a celebrity. Jesus' kingdom is about mercy for sinners, hope for the poor, and liberation for the oppressed. But the most important part is—it's not about me. It's not about what I can get from the world, but rather about what I can give to the world. It's what I can sacrifice of myself in order to enrich the community. And that can be threatening. That kind of idea can get a person killed.

Am I willing to humble myself in order to serve others? Am I willing to make myself vulnerable to those who might take advantage of me or not appreciate me? Am I willing to take a public stand against violence or injustice, even if it means that I might lose my job or my friends? I would like to say "yes," but I am too often willing just to "go along." And that's how I deny Jesus—by denying what he stood for, what he sacrificed his life for. That's how we all might deny Jesus as a society, convinced that his vision for us threatens the status quo, and threatens the country or national security.

Caiaphas was prophetic when he said, "It's better for one man to die for the people than for the entire nation to perish." The trouble is, we forget that when we allow an innocent person to die, we sacrifice our own souls. In a dangerous game of spiritual chess, that is a killing move. Check the king, then checkmate. But we had forgot what God meant by kingship.

So we killed the wrong king. We checkmated ourselves. Checkmate.

What will God do now?

Holy Saturday

God's Strategy

Today we stand at the foot of the cross. We are both disciple and betrayer. We want to be a loyal follower, not part of the riotous crowd. But Jesus keeps giving us signs pointing to a different destination, and we aren't paying attention. The sinner is not the hooker downtown, or the unethical mortgage broker, or that arrogant dictator on the other side of the world. It's you. It's me. We are "those people." We didn't pay attention because we committed the more subtle sins of denial, arrogance, and indifference.

I think of Brian, who thirteen years ago committed a nonviolent sexual offense. He was on probation, but today he is free—in a way. He is shunned by everyone. No one will rent a place to him. He has to admit he committed a felony, and he cannot find a job because no one will hire him. Without a job, he can't find a place to live. Because he doesn't earn any money, he is always hungry. He is considered dirt. Not dust, like "remember that you are dust," but dirt. Worthless, bad, unforgivable. It's been thirteen years, and he has done nothing wrong since then. He has been trying to become a productive citizen, if only we would let him. He is continually punished by the justice system and hated by society. Because of his offense, he does not command our sympathy; in fact we often think he deserves the abusive treatment he receives from us.

But Brian is still a human being and a beloved child of God. God loves him. And Jesus forgives him. Why can't we?

We continue to crucify those for whom Christ was crucified—the poor, the sick, the oppressed, those in prison, the hungry, the homeless, people who look suspicious or different from us—and even those who did offend but have "served their time." For some of those people, their time never ends, because we continue to punish them.

Maybe we have judged Brian unworthy of our time or support, compassion or respect. Maybe I judge whole groups, whole communities—the poor, the ex-offenders—as undeserving of love, or even of a sustainable life. By my lack of sympathy, I let them languish, walking downtown in their shabby clothes and donated shoes that don't fit. They can't earn a decent living, they can't find housing, they have to walk miles to get dinner, to find water to drink, to go to the bathroom. I crucify them little by little, through my neglect and my uncaring. I turn my head, I don't look at them, and they can't see into my eyes. I don't speak to them, get to know them, find out how I might help.

Love's strategy—so profoundly articulated by Jesus' life— is a hard strategy, but it takes us deep into the heart of God. Love's strategy will ultimately win. Tonight, we will see the light triumph over the darkness. And if we look at the heart of our faith, we will see that love's strategy has always won. It is a strategy rooted in forgiveness and healing. Jesus never swerved from love's strategy, even at the end. Bleeding on the cross, he prayed, "Father, forgive them. They don't know what they're doing." He knows God's strategy well, he knows what the prophets have said over and over again, like Ezekiel, who said, "God does not desire the death of sinners." God desires liberation from oppression—even the oppression of an empire that killed the Son of God.

But love's strategy will win. Because God isn't about power. That person on the cross is the face and embodiment of God's great love and desire for each of us. Now it's time for us to take him down from the cross, to take all crucified people down from the cross—for love's sake. And for Brian's sake, too.

Easter Day

The Wonder of Resurrection: A Triumph of Humility

The birth of Christ came at night—a night filled with the soft haze of stars about to break with the song of angels, a luminous brightness—a "silent night." It was God's time—a mystical time of mystery and wonder and awe. The staggering truth was born on that night: God's infinite love for us comes to be born among us as an impossibly tiny baby, and so we are not afraid.

In the Incarnation, God showed that God believes in us humans enough to come live with us. God is not ashamed of us, even as we fret and worry and admit our wickedness. God honors our humanity, because in our truest and deepest selves, we have the capacity to love, to trust, and to hope.

The Resurrection of Christ came in the very early morning—after a dark and somber night, a quiet morning without song or talk or hope—only tears. In this early morning, it is easy to shed tears of loss. After this season of Lent, we no longer have Jesus at our side helping us grow up in faith.

But it's God's time again, though no one knows it yet. The somber angel (no trumpets or hosts this time) reminds us, "Do not be afraid." The same mystery and magic of God's timeline tingles our hearts but in a different key than at Christmas. This is a different kind of mystery and a different wonder and awe, filled instead with fear, bewilderment, and disbelief. God's power is clear, raising Jesus from the dead, and it is a fearsome power. As with the birth of Jesus, we are shown God's deep, deep love for us.

God still believes in us, despite our betrayals. Despite our act in snuffing out Jesus' humanity, God still honors our humanity. Despite our denial of Jesus' love for us, God still loves us.

God raises up Jesus from the dead. God triumphs—not with the power of force and tyranny, but with the power of humility and forgiveness, compassion, mercy, and the greatest power of all—love. The morning has broken, the news has broken, and we—the broken, beautiful, and beloved—are risen to new life as well.

Alleulua! Christ is risen!

About the Author

Joanna Leiserson is an Episcopal priest in the Diocese of Southern Ohio. She has served at Christ Church Cathedral, Cincinnati, as canon for formation and mission, and at St. Anne Episcopal Church, West Chester, Ohio, as interim rector.

Joanna has a deep passion for Christian formation, seen as the formation of the whole person as a follower of God, and as the formation of a whole people as participants in creating God's new creation, the reign of God on earth. To this end, she is also a passionate advocate for social and economic justice, that we might be healers for the brokenhearted, bearers of hope to the poor, and tireless voices against oppression and injustice.

Other loves include astronomy, paleontology, history, natural history, the wonders of God's creation and God's creatures, and the astonishing beauty of the English language.

Joanna has three grown children and at least three grown cats. She is also the author of *Weaving God's Promises: A Curriculum for Children in The Episcopal Church* and a contributor to *Meeting God Day by Day*, published by Forward Movement.